APPRECIATING ALL RELIGIONS

Religious Literacy In Small Bites

Paramjit Singh Sachdeva

authorHOUSE®

AuthorHouse™
1663 Liberty Drive
Bloomington, IN 47403
www.authorhouse.com
Phone: 1-800-839-8640

First published by AuthorHouse 3/11/2011

ISBN: 978-1-4567-2111-4 (e)
ISBN: 978-1-4567-2112-1 (sc)

Library of Congress Control Number: 2010919233

Printed in the United States of America

Contents

Part One
Our Religions, Past and Present

Part Two
Religious Diversity, Unity, and Interaction

Dedication

To my parents

Maj. Sudarshan Singh Sachdeva
and Mrs. Narindar Kaur Sachdeva

My wife's parents

Bakshi Hardev Singh
and Mrs. Nirmal Bakshi

And my grandparents

S. Mohan Singh Kalra
and Mrs. Mohinder Kaur Kalra

For showing the way

Acknowledgements

THIS BOOK IS by and for a layperson interested in learning about others' religions. This topic has the potential to inadvertently rub people on the wrong side, so in order to get the key facts right, I have consulted a number of scholarly sources. These are listed in the Select Bibliography; and I gratefully acknowledge their huge contribution to this work.

I have been encouraged by readers of my book *Appreciating Sikhism* to write another one. In writing this book, I have been inspired also by members of my own multi-religious family—starting with my grandparents, and continuing to my children's generation—who have shown undeniably how necessary and gratifying it is to respect religions other than one's own. They have shown by personal example that treating others as you yourself wish to be treated is always the best policy, as is taught in the sacred scriptures of all our religions.

At the personal level, I am most grateful to my wife Nona (Anju) Sachdeva for her tremendous loving support on the most important aspects of life, and when I need it most; and to my son Bikram and daughter Nidhi for their openness to different cultures and religions, and for serving as sounding boards at different stages of this project.

Margaret Michna, Catherine Davis, and other members of the design team at AuthorHouse have provided guidance and technical support when needed, and have helped produce a book that I hope will serve its readers well.

The errors of omission and commission that remain are my own, and I would be happy to correct them as appropriate.

Paramjit Singh Sachdeva
Vienna, Virginia

Preface

WHAT A DIFFERENCE only 5,000 years can make. Look back to just 3000 BCE. Globally, there was a great variety of tribal cults and cultures, with innumerable gods and religions, but relatively little religious conflict. Mankind, by present standards, was "uncivilized." Fast forward now to the present time. For most humans, there is now *only one* God. There are far fewer living religions, civilization is widespread, but religious conflicts abound. How did this come about? And importantly, how should we deal with our irreducible religious diversity, before a global "clash of civilizations" and endemic religious intolerance engulf us all?

In exploring such questions, we note that religious diversity is not new. There were countless religions during pre-history. The humans who formed our first civilizations worshipped a wide variety of gods, and had diverse religious beliefs and practices. These religions had much in common, but were different too in many ways. The archeological and other evidence painstakingly unearthed over centuries and recent anthropological studies of so-called primitive societies have established this beyond doubt.

Most ancient religions left no indelible mark on the historical record, but some did, and contributed to new faiths that then took root. All religions gradually evolved over time, and in so doing helped shape human history. In turn, religions too have been shaped by political, social, and cultural contexts that have drawn people together or driven them apart. The two-way interplay of faith and history has varied from place to place, and has naturally led to a wide range of religions and sects.

Throughout human history, religion has mattered. It has satisfied a uniquely-human need for connecting with God, the universe, and eternity. It has served also to connect us with our innermost spiritual self, and with fellow man. Religion has been a force for the good, but it has also been a source of much misery. Millions have died for and because of their religion. Armies on both sides of a religious conflict have claimed that they were both serving (the same) God. Ironically, we ourselves—with God's grace—had been inspired to create some of the key religious differences that had led to these disputes.

Many of us value our own religion, but know little and care even less about other religions. In an increasingly inter-connected world, such ignorance is inexcusable and potentially dangerous. To facilitate religious literacy and a better appreciation of all religions, this book provides a perspective on how our thirteen living religions came into being, how they developed, and what they have become. If we could graciously accept that religious unity and diversity are God-inspired *and* man-made—in accordance with *our own God's* Will that we presumably seek to honor—we could perhaps live in greater harmony with each other, despite our religious differences.

All religions are complex and multifaceted, and have evolved over time. Many volumes are needed to do each full justice; and a comprehensive in-depth coverage of every religion is beyond the scope and purpose of this small book. Instead, it covers salient aspects of each religion's creation and evolution, focusing on key beliefs and practices. Since the canvas is broad and the time-frame long, only some aspects are highlighted, and details are omitted. All living religions are covered, to varying extent. We examine, from a believer's point of view, whether all religions are in essence the same; and note key differences. The purpose is to better appreciate the unity as well as diversity of our religious traditions, and not to deprecate any religion in any way.

The book is based on others' scholarly work, but I express my lay opinion, recognizing that others may see religious unity and diversity differently. To make the main message and storyline clearer for the intended non-academic audience, selectivity is unavoidable. If I inadvertently omit a key feature or misrepresent any aspect of any religion, I seek the reader's indulgence, since the possible errors of omission and commission are entirely unintended. I wish simply to provoke further thought and understanding, and leave the rest to you.

Part One

Our Religions, Past and Present

Chapter 1

In the Beginning

GOD, THE CREATOR, made the universe more than thirteen billion years ago. Humans came much later. Still, we have been in existence for perhaps a few million years, the last fifty thousand or so as modern humans. Regrettably, our archeological record goes back only about fifteen thousand years to the earliest human settlements, and our written history covers only the most recent five thousand years.

For the past five millennia and possibly longer, humans have been religious. We have had many gods and a variety of beliefs, many of which no longer exist. Now, most humans believe in one God—the all-powerful and loving Creator—and in one of a dozen or so living faiths.

The story of each religion is different, in terms of how it was created and how it evolved. The gods of the Greeks and Romans, of the Vedic Aryans, and of the Mayans and Aztecs left their mark on the gods that followed. So did the religions of antiquity in Mesopotamia, Egypt, the Indus Valley, the Far East, Meso-America and elsewhere. In many instances, somewhat similar features emerged independently at different places and at different times, driven by God's grace and inspiration, and human needs and expectations.

Of the current religions with a global presence, only Zoroastrianism, Judaism, and Hinduism can be traced back to the 2nd millennium BCE or earlier. Five religions—Jainism, Buddhism, Confucianism, Taoism, and Shintoism—emerged from new founders or existing traditions during the next one thousand years. Two more major religions—Christianity and Islam, the two largest in the world today—were created during the 1st millennium CE by two new prophets who revealed new messages from God. And three more religions—Sikhism, the Mormon Church, and the Baha'i Faith—were revealed to their founders in the 2nd millennium of the Common Era (CE), with the latter two emerging as recently as less than two hundred years ago.

Our earliest living religions were inspired by various notions of the supernatural, and built on indigenous religious and cultural traditions that preceded them. As new religions emerged, they introduced new notions of the divine and how to reach Him, as revealed or inspired by God. Religious inspiration came also from fresh opportunities for interchange of peoples and ideas, as all religions interacted with those that existed by their side. Some ideas were incorporated with little change, others after considerable debate and re-interpretation over long periods of time. The various religions influenced each others' myths, beliefs, practices, and rituals—leading to many common features as well as differences.

Throughout these years, all religions continued to grow and evolve, to a greater or lesser extent, and became what they are today. Every living religion is thus the result of both continuity and change spanning hundreds of years and incorporating the revealed message of its founding prophet(s) and the inspired spiritual wisdom of many mystics, sages, saints, and seers. All religions have also been sustained by the unheralded contributions of numerous ordinary folk who enabled these religions to remain alive and oftentimes thrive, simply by being faithful followers through times good and bad.

How these thirteen religions were formed and subsequently evolved is the subject of Part One of this book. Only major milestones are mentioned and details are deliberately omitted, to enable the big picture and underlying patterns to present themselves. What these religions have in common and how they differ, and how we could take account of this unity and diversity are covered in Part Two.

Some similarities and differences can be pre-viewed in Part One too—for the unity and diversity of religions are the natural outcome of the many different paths these religions have taken during their complex and occasionally hard-to-discern processes of creation and evolution. The separation of some of these interlinked ideas into the various chapters of the book does, however, serve a purpose. The fascinating stories of our living religions can be outlined and the overall pattern comprehended more easily, and we can more-conveniently address an inherently-complicated subject by reducing its big pieces to bite size.

INDIGENOUS TRADITIONS

WE DO NOT know much about indigenous traditions of the ancient past, but from the religions of indigenous peoples who have survived into the modern era, we can infer that traditional beliefs were closely intertwined with the local society and culture and with man's understanding of himself, nature, the super-natural, and how these interacted. In pre-literate societies, religion found expression through art and architecture—through painting, music, dance, costumes, and sculpture. Some of these we can still see.

In Africa, the cradle of mankind, indigenous traditions naturally varied from place to place. They often included belief in a supreme reality, other gods, ancestor worship, and the practice of magic. The pygmies believed in a benevolent god of the forest, the east-Africans in a god of the open skies, and the west-Africans had a variety of cults of nature spirits and ancestors. Some pan-African beliefs were associated with "mother" earth and life-giving water and other natural phenomena. All these attested to the connection between man, nature, and the gods and spirits that took care of the living and the dead. There were many kinds of rituals, initiation ceremonies, magical objects and superstitions, and medicine men with material and spiritual powers. Intricate masks, carvings, and sculpture represented the powers of ancestors and spirits over the living members of the tribe or community.

On the Indian sub-continent in Asia, nomadic

bands of hunters and gatherers had both survival and the supernatural in mind as they roamed the forests and plains. As in Africa, theirs was a holistic view of the world of humans, nature and gods—with the gods affecting human fate as part of the natural order. Deities were of various kinds: general and local, male and female, approachable and remote. Benevolent female deities were associated with food and fertility, male deities with the powerful forces of nature. Ancestor spirits and cultish clan-deities catered to local needs, and some could be approached directly while others required priests as intermediaries. The spirit outlived the human body, and joined other spirits. Religion was multi-faceted, with a mix of myths and ceremonies, priests and seers, sacrifices and offerings, and sacred rituals, sounds, objects, times, and places.

In East Asia too, the rites and rituals were diverse, as were the modes of sacrifice and worship. The means for communicating with the spirits and the supernatural also varied. The deities were many and served specific functions, such as reproduction and overcoming disease. The ancestral spirits mattered, and priests and shamans guided practices both mundane and sacred. When people lived in small hamlets near lakes, ponds and trees—and guarded turf and tribe with everything they had, including their special gods—indigenous religions were local. But the general idea was the same: the gods cared about what happened to you, and could be propitiated with the right rites, priests and prayers, shamans and séances, and sacrifices and gifts of various kinds.

In Central Asia, pastoral tribes developed their own pantheon of gods and ways of reaching them. In some cases, their mythology spoke of a good celestial being who reigned supreme in the highest sky, and of a mythical evil spirit that dwelled in the depths of the underworld. The celestial creator was all-powerful, all-wise, creative, caring, and benevolent. Subordinate to him were lesser gods and sons and messengers who resided in the lower heavens, watching over and helping humans on earth. The supreme deity was confronted with the forces of evil, but ultimately prevailed.

In Australia, indigenous beliefs of the aborigines made no sharp distinction between the sacred and the secular. As in the mythical past or eternal dreamtime, the supernatural was natural. There was a variety of beliefs: supernatural beings emerged from their sleep to take physical shape but retained the powers of the spirits; life persisted in different forms, and death was merely a transition; well-being in the afterlife was not influenced by the quality of life that had preceded it; and rituals associated with death ensured that the spirits of ancestors had safe passage and did not return to trouble the living. Underlying all this, man and nature were one.

In the Americas, religions displayed resemblances, as well as variety. In all known religions, cosmic phenomena were interrelated, and religious and social aspects of society were interwoven. The Aztecs and the Mayans distinguished between the ancient and the more recent gods. The Aztec goddess of the earth was the "mother" of the gods, and there were gods and goddesses of rain, wind, fire, sky, sun, sexuality, fertility, war, maize, and hunting, among others. Some gods were associated with particular occupational groups, such as merchants or mosaic workers. Different social classes and groups—nobility, military, priests, merchants, craftsmen, commoners, servants, and slaves—worshiped or gave prominence to different gods, and celebrated a variety of religious festivals. Human and animal sacrifice was performed to please the gods who had created humans and retained an interest in their welfare.

Mayan gods included the creator couple and gods of the sun, earth, wind, water, and fertility, as well as of maize, music, hearth, flower, drink, medicine, and many others. In contrast, the creator god of the Andean people was indivisible and supreme, and the other deities were his sons and daughters and their descendents. Some of these gods were good, and others were evil powers, including the gods of death and destruction. There was belief in an afterlife, mummification, and sun worship.

In Europe too, the religious beliefs of indigenous groups were similar in many ways to those elsewhere, yet different in other ways. In some communities, the sky-god controlled the sun and lightning, and there were other major deities and lesser gods and goddesses. There were gods for war, earth, sea, storm, fertility, sexual love, magic and divination, arts and crafts, and healing, to mention just a few. The supernatural and human constantly interacted in myths, magic, portents, and cult practices, and some animals had supernatural significance.

In many religions, priests and cult leaders preserved and transmitted myths, legends, tribal history and law; and they also organized sacrifices, interpreted omens, and conducted magical rites and elaborate rituals. Some cults practiced magic, others offered men and horses and other animals as sacrifice, and some others believed in the afterlife, including a belief that the soul passes to another body. In some cults, the dead were believed to live on in their graves with the goods buried with them, and ancestors bestowed prosperity and wisdom on the living.

Examples of indigenous religions can thus be found in far-off places on every continent around the globe. Some general observations can be cautiously made about these religions despite the understandable paucity of hard evidence.

Overall, mankind's inner search for meaning and for a connection with some form of a Supreme Reality (God) as well as with other gods were common to many cults, tribes, and larger social groups. Ideas about the mundane and the sacred were reflected in myths, symbols, and beliefs about the gods and how we could reach them. The gods were interested in man's welfare, and responded to his offerings, rituals, and prayers. The sacred was within reach, and could be grasped by the holy.

Some beliefs and practices of particular indigenous communities resembled, to varying extent, the traditional religious beliefs on other continents, even though they had developed independently. Noticeable differences existed too. Despite their variety, all religious beliefs and practices were believed to find favor with the spirits and the supernatural, and presumably served their respective communities equally well.

Mankind's indigenous religions were thus, in a sense, "separate but equal." Such is the marvel of human nature, especially when it relates to the gods. This was before the advent of civilization on a large scale, and the further evolution of these religions.

RELIGIONS OF ANTIQUITY

INITIALLY, INDIGENOUS COMMUNITIES were small and isolated, scattered but numerous. Each had its own distinctive religious traditions. As they grew and began to interact with other communities through social, economic and political ties, reciprocal sharing and mutual influence were inevitable. The pattern that emerged varied from place to place. Though the available archeological record of these exchanges is spotty and incomplete, it does provide evidence of human development that was significant, continuous, and widespread, especially around the large river systems where settled agriculture could be practiced and large populations could be sustained.

As major centers of civilization arose around the rivers Nile, Euphrates, and the Indus, for example, so did more complex systems of religious belief and practice. These religions served both as a binding force for the community and as an expression of their creative aspirations and increasingly sophisticated speculations about the unknown. As a result, the previous religious traditions changed, some dramatically and others incrementally and cumulatively. By the time the major civilizations that we have now unearthed reached their peaks and then declined, the earlier indigenous traditions had been lost forever, leaving behind only the archeological record of what they had once been.

Some of these civilizations existed about five thousand years ago. They provide the starting point for a deeper appreciation of what we now call religions of antiquity—for even these "new" religions were subsequently transformed into or displaced by the thirteen still-newer major faiths that exist today.

The selected aspects briefly outlined below are meant only to be illustrative of the kinds of beliefs and practices that existed just a few millennia ago.

The Mesopotamian Civilization. Mesopotamia, in the ancient Near East along the banks of the rivers Tigris and Euphrates, was a mixing bowl of races and cultures, home to the Sumerians, Babylonians, Assyrians, and others. The ordered components of the universe—sky, earth, heaven, spirits, among others—revealed the divine mind and shaped life on earth. The excavated remains of deities, shrines, sacred figurines, and places and customs of burial and sacrifice show an awareness of the natural and supernatural forces on which existence depended.

The gods were immortal, but lived as humans did—they ate, drank, married, had children, and resided in dwellings with their possessions. They had specialized functions too, for example, Anu, the heaven god, originally ruled supreme over a pantheon of gods; Enlil was lord of the atmosphere, sun, moon, and vegetation; and Enki was the god of wisdom who made humans aware of divine plans. His son Marduk later headed the Babylonian pantheon. Enlil, the offspring of the first divine pair, Enki and Ninki, possessed tablets by which human fate was determined.

With the passage of time, the gods changed; and they changed places with each other as well. In heaven, as on earth. By the middle of the 2nd millennium BCE, the god Enlil was replaced by Marduk in Babylonia and Ashur in Assyria. Marduk was later greeted as Bel (or Baal), the supreme god. Enlil's consort Ninlil was identified with the Sumerian goddess Innin and the Babylonian goddess Ishtar, who gradually absorbed the functions of earlier female deities. As the goddess of love and fertility, Ishar was known to Syrians as Anat, to Arabs as Atar, to Greeks as Astarte, and to Egyptians as Isis.

The seven major deities of the assembly of gods were supported by fifty other great gods and spirits, each with different functions and attributes. Some gods came down to earth, and like humans they needed to be fed the choicest meat from sacrifices and clothed with fresh ornaments and garments for particular festivals. Individuals invoked them in prayers, sometimes through intercessory deities, and worshiped them with hymns which extolled divine attributes and achievements.

The errors and sins to be avoided were listed in all areas of daily living, with the penalties specified in terms of sickness, trouble, and even death. The results of favorable action too were recorded by the gods, and were duly rewarded. The gods' wishes could be divined and understood through signs and omens; but truth and justice were the collective responsibility of gods, kings, and ordinary men and women, since the whole of life was one unified religious exercise.

All this, and a lot more about the cosmos and the underlying basis of man's religious beliefs, was made known through mythological legends, including the Sumerian story that the god Ea and the goddess Aruru created man from clay by the power of the divine word. Both the epics of Gilgamesh and Atrahasis introduced "the Flood" as a divine judgment on humankind. In each, the god Enki (Ea) warned an especially-chosen man to build a boat to save his family and all animals; and the vessel later landed on Mount Nisir.

The Mesopotamian view of death and the afterlife was reasonably clear as well. The dead were judged by the Sun god and by Nannar who decreed their lot, which depended on how life had been lived. Since the king was the vice-regent of the gods on earth, royalty expected to be treated well in the hereafter. The royal graves at Ur (c. 2600 BCE) included some of their followers, musicians, gifts of jewelry, vessels and musical instruments, and draught animals.

The Nile Valley Civilization. In ancient Egypt too, the tombs were called houses of eternity, and pyramids provided comfortable homes for royalty during their afterlife. Preservation of the body was important, so the dead were buried, not cremated. There were several creation myths, and the gods responsible for creation had pride of place in the pantheon. The primal creator-god was Atum, also identified as the sun-god Re, who had come into existence by himself, and had by himself created his offspring. Gods were associated with natural phenomena: the sun, the Nile, crocodiles, and others. The world was created by god's intelligence and implemented by his spoken word; and living beings were originally made from clay, using a potter's wheel.

Eventually, the god Osiris emerged from relative obscurity to great importance in the funerary cult. The pharaoh was the son of the sun god Re, and by becoming Osiris, the dead pharaoh ruled over the dead. Some Gods were depicted as animals or as humans with an animal head. The pharaoh himself was officially a god, and some prominent persons were similarly deified after death.

There were triads of gods too: of a god, his spouse, and his son; and in some cases the trinity was regarded as one.

Fire was used in ritual worship of the statue of a god in the inner sanctuary, where the priest offered sacrifices and adorned it with garments and insignia. During festivals, mythological stories were enacted in drama, and gods and their consorts and sons were carried in processions. The gods died and were reborn, as did humans; so dead bodies were buried. There was belief in judgment after death, and if the verdict was favorable, eternal happiness was assured. The soul's external manifestation could be transformed after death, allowing it to emerge at will from the tomb. The moral virtues emphasized as part of religion included good conduct, truth, justice, wisdom, charity, humility, patience, and self-restraint.

Greco-Roman Civilizations. The ancient Greek pantheon was very different from the ancient Egyptian pantheon, though only a small sea separated the two societies. The Greeks gave prominence to a fertility goddess, known by a variety of names: the Great Mother, Mother of Gods, Ishtar, Rhea, and Ma. The mother goddess often had a consort; in Crete for example, by the second millennium BCE, the consort Zeus, born on Mount Ida. Later, Zeus was known as the universal supreme god, father of gods and of men. Over time, the gods of Greece and other gods were repositioned, some gaining more power and others disappearing entirely from the pantheon. In addition, as was the case for peoples of other ancient civilizations, the power and sacredness of nature was recognized, and there were gods of the sun, moon, sky, and rivers, as well as rituals for purification and holiness.

The Greeks recognized a universal supreme god, and Zeus was the god of righteousness. During the first millennium BCE, many cults of various kinds emerged; and in one such cult, man was believed to consist of both body and spirit; and there was a doctrine of reincarnation through a sorrowful circle of death and rebirth, from which only the proper initiation ceremonies offered escape.

Ancient Rome emphasized underworld anthropomorphic deities with specialized functions, and there was preoccupation with the afterlife. Ancestral spirits initially related to field and farm, then took on human-like personalities, and later became gods, who further changed upon contact with the Greek gods. Jupiter, the supreme god of the Roman pantheon was originally a sky-god, who was later identified with the Greek god Zeus. Religious festivals, sacrifices, and rituals secured the favor of the gods—provided the prescribed taboos and restrictions were followed, precise formulas were recited, and the proper sacrifices were made. Emperors were worshiped in life, and the good ones were deified after death. Belief in astrology, magic, sorcery, and witchcraft was common, as was fear of eternal punishment beyond the grave.

The Persian Civilization. In ancient Persia, before or during the second millennium BCE, the nomadic warlike Aryans had come from the east and northwest to occupy the land. The sun god was the chief supporter of the supreme deity Ahura Mazda in his struggle against the forces of darkness and evil. Mithras was the savior-god, the spirit of the firmament, and ally of the good god Ahura Mazda. Other religious beliefs in the western region of Persia were influenced by Mesopotamia, Greece and Rome; and in the eastern region by India and even China.

The Indus Valley Civilization. The Indus civilization flourished between 2600-1900 BCE. In the Indus valley, Aryan beliefs centered around Vedic gods and sacred hymns and rituals. There were many gods, including gods of the sun, moon, storms, and other natural elements. The prescribed rituals included fire worship and animal sacrifices. Professional priests chanted holy sounds, religious ceremonies and festivals abounded, seers and sages and myths and superstition were highly regarded, and the common man was content to follow the rituals prescribed by tradition.

Thus, looking back to our ancient civilizations, we note that belief in some kind of religion was universal. Though few tangible traces of previous religious traditions had remained, their deep moral imprint had lingered in our earliest civilizations. There was a stunning variety of gods and religious beliefs and practices around the globe; but these religions had many common features too. There was noticeable continuity of religious thought and behavior, as well as continual change, right up to our recent past, a few thousand years ago.

Both the universality of religion and the diverse forms it took simply reflected our common humanity and our basic human nature. It would have been odd indeed if the similarity of functions that religion served and the diversity of its expression had been absent. After all, humans are the same everywhere, and yet are obviously different. Universality does not imply identity, especially in relation to our religions, past or present.

Our Living Religions

FAST-FORWARD NOW TO current times. The numerous religions of antiquity are no more, and have been replaced by or transformed into just thirteen major living religions—*none* of which existed a mere five thousand years ago. Our newest religions are introduced below.

Zoroastrianism. Zoroastrianism is the oldest of our revealed, creedal religions. It emerged during the 2nd millennium BCE from the Bronze Age culture and indigenous traditions of settled pastoralists on the Inner Asian steppes surrounding the Caspian Sea. The religion owes its origin to the prophet Zoroaster, whose hymns to the God *Ahura Mazda* are recorded as the *Gathas* in the *Avesta*, the religion's sacred scripture. Zoroastrianism was once dominant in Persia and Asia Minor, but now has only a few million followers, mostly in India and Iran.

The Abrahamic Religions. There are five such religions: the three main Abrahamic religions—Judaism, Christianity, and Islam—and the Mormon Church and the Baha'i Faith which trace their roots respectively to Christianity and Islam.

Judaism is the oldest of the Abrahamic religions, and is based on the revelations communicated by *Yahweh* (God) to the prophets Abraham, Noah, and Moses, among others. The Jewish scripture, known as the *Hebrew Bible*, includes the *Torah* and the *Talmud*. Judaism does not seek to convert others; and has more than 13 million followers worldwide. The majority of Jews live in North America; and most of the remaining are in Israel and Europe. Judaism gave rise to Christianity and Islam, the two largest religions in the world today. Its influence on the history of world religions and political events in Europe and the Middle East is perhaps unmatched.

Christianity is today the largest religion in the world, with over two billion followers. It was founded by The Lord Jesus Christ (the Messiah) and his immediate disciples in Jerusalem. Christians believe in the *New Testament* of Jesus Christ, as well as the *Old Testament*, which is part of the Hebrew Bible. Christianity spread throughout the Mediterranean region and Europe during the first one thousand years of the Common Era. The majority of Christians today are in the Americas and Africa, the result of aggressive colonization and proselytizing by Europeans during the 15th to 19th centuries. Most other Christians are in Europe, Australia, and some countries in East Asia.

Islam was founded by the prophet Muhammad in 610 CE in Mecca, on the Arabian Peninsula. Muslims— meaning those who submit to the will of *Allah* (God)— follow God's message as revealed to Prophet Muhammad and recorded in the *Holy Qur'an*, Islam's sacred scripture. Initially, the rapid geographical spread of Islam throughout the Middle East, North Africa, and Asia was the result of active conversion, conquest, and trade. There are now over one billion Muslims, mostly in Asia, Africa, and the Middle East, though there are many Muslims in Europe and other parts of the world too. Islam is one of the two most-significant religions in the world today, the other being Christianity.

The Mormon Church was founded by the prophet Joseph Smith in New York state (USA) in 1830 CE; and the Baha'i faith was founded by the prophet Baha'u'llah in Persia (Iran) in 1863 CE. Mormons follow the *Christian Bible* as well as the *Book of Mormon*, which was revealed to prophet Joseph Smith; and the Baha'i follow the teachings of the *Qur'an* as well as the *Book of Certitude*, which was revealed to prophet Baha'u'llah. Mormon and Baha'i communities are now established in many countries, the result of evangelical missions that seek to bring God's latest messages to mankind across the globe.

The Indic Religions. The four "Indic" religions—Hinduism, Jainism, Buddhism, and Sikhism—were founded on the Indian sub-continent. All these religions believe in the unending cycle of rebirth (*samsara*). They believe also in the moral law of *karma* that says that all actions have consequences that then need to be worked out during the present or future lives. The reincarnation of the soul (*atman*) delays the attainment of *moksha* (freedom from rebirth) which is the ultimate goal, and thus may seem like an unending punishment for past sins. But it also ensures that everyone gets many more than a single opportunity to get it right.

The Indic religions have many differences too. Hinduism and Sikhism believe in a transcendent God (the Creator), respectively known to them as *Brahman* and *Waheguru*; but Hindus, unlike Sikhs, also believe in incarnations (*avatars*) of God, in the form of gods and goddesses who periodically come into this world to help mankind. In contrast, Buddhists and Jains do not believe in a transcendent God. They were asked by their faith's founder(s) to rely only on themselves and on the teachings of their religion. These founders had originally created non-theistic religions, though they themselves are now sometimes worshiped as God.

Hinduism does not have an identifiable founder or prophet. Instead, it traces its roots to the inspired sayings of sages and seers that were preserved and transmitted orally for many centuries, and then were recorded in the *Vedas*. Now there are many sacred Hindu texts written during the course of many centuries, including the *Puranas* and the *Upanishads*, of which the better known are the *Mahabharata*, the *Bhagavad Gita*, and the *Ramayana*. Religious practices and rituals are numerous and diverse as well. Hinduism has evolved into a very complex and diverse religion that is as much a "way of life" as a faith based on firmly-set beliefs or doctrine. It has long been the dominant religion of the Indian sub-continent, where about one billion Hindus now live. Hinduism does not believe in conversion and has not spread by conquest, so the large number of Hindus today is due to natural population growth over the millennia.

Jainism was founded by Mahavira Jain, the 24th Great Teacher (or Ford-builder, *Tirthankara*), during the sixth century BCE in northeastern India. Jains emphasize ascetic non-violence as taught and practiced by their Tirthankaras. Their scriptures include the *Puravas* (the Old Texts) and the *Tattavarthasutra*, which outline the path to spiritual liberation.

Buddhism was founded by Gautama Buddha who attained enlightenment in 528 BCE in the same region of northeastern India where Mahavira Jain had achieved liberation from the cycle of rebirth. Buddhist sacred texts include the *Tipitaka* (the Pali canon) and the *Prajnaparamita* (or Perfection of Wisdom). Buddhism focuses primarily on meditation and the Middle Way taught by the Buddha; but has also developed other branches that have different beliefs and practices than those originally taught by the Buddha.

Jainism and Buddhism flourished in India alongside Hinduism for over fifteen hundred years. By the thirteenth century CE, with the resurgence of Hinduism and the advent of Islam in India, Buddhism was displaced to neighboring countries. Though it virtually vanished from India, in succeeding centuries it became popular in modified form in Sri Lanka, East Asia, Tibet, China, and Japan. There are now perhaps more than three hundred million Buddhists in these and other parts of the world.

In contrast, Jainism did not spread beyond India's borders. It has remained closely-tied to the teachings of Mahavira Jain; and, like Buddhism, does not seek to convert others. Some Jain communities outside India have begun sharing temples with Hindus, but this is more for pragmatic than doctrinal reasons. Their rites and rituals, though sometimes patterned on Vedic or Buddhist practices, are still driven by the doctrines of their founder, and are not directed toward Hindu deities or the Buddha's teachings. There are now about five million Jains, mostly in India.

Sikhism is a relatively young religion; and was founded by Guru Nanak in 1499 CE in the Punjab state of northern India. Sikhs believe in the revelations of *Waheguru* (the Almighty God) to the prophet Guru Nanak and his nine successor Gurus, which are now enshrined in the Sikhs' sacred scripture, the *Guru Granth Sahib*. They worship God's Word (*shabad*) as communicated to their Gurus, are tolerant of other religions, and do not believe in proselytizing. Sikhism is the fifth largest religion in the world, with about twenty-three million followers, mostly in India. During the past century, Sikhs have settled in countries around the globe in search of economic opportunities.

The East Asian Religions. These cover the three religions—Confucianism, Taoism, and Shintoism—that were founded in China and other countries of East Asia. These religions are closely related to each other, as well as to Buddhism. They are predominant mainly in China and Japan, but their influence and ancient teachings are gradually spreading around the globe.

Confucianism is based on the teachings of the sage Confucius who lived in China from 551 BCE to 479 BCE. The religion does not rely on a Supreme Being, focusing instead on moral values and ritualistic practices that lead to a harmonious society. Confucianism was the dominant religion of China for more than two millennia, but was temporarily eclipsed by Communism during the latter half of the twentieth century CE. It is now making a comeback, both at the individual level and as a state-sponsored ethical code of conduct and values. It is difficult to know how many of the 1.2 billion Chinese live by Confucian norms and values, but the number is very large.

Taoism and Shintoism are mainly followed in China and Japan respectively. They combine elements of indigenous cultural and religious traditions with Confucianism and Buddhism. Followers of Taoism and Shintoism value peace of mind, practice a variety of rites and rituals, and seek to live in harmony with nature, which they revere and worship in many different ways. They do not seek to convert others; but their numbers are substantial, especially in China and Japan.

We begin our review of these thirteen religions with

Zoroastrianism, arguably the oldest of our living religions. Subsequent chapters then cover the other living religions in rough chronological order of the date of their creation. Brief outlines of each religion are given, covering their creation and evolution, key beliefs and practices, and the main branches or sects that have developed over time.

These summaries seek to enhance religious literacy; and are intended to be informative, not comprehensive or exhaustive. They set the stage for a discussion in Part Two of the book of religious diversity, unity, interfaith interactions, and a promising perspective that encourages respectful acceptance—or at the very least, respectful tolerance—of *all* our living religions.

Chapter 2

Zoroastrianism

CREATION AND EVOLUTION

ZOROASTRIANISM WAS FIRST preached by the prophet Zarathushtra (Zoroaster in Greek) who lived in Persia (Iran) about 3,500 years ago. This was when the first *Rigvedic* hymns that later evolved into Brahmanic Hinduism on the Indian subcontinent were being composed. The Old Avestan language of the prophet Zarathushtra was close to the Vedic tongue, thus allowing us to date the origins of Zoroastrianism.

Zoraoaster built on the traditions of the proto-Indo-Iranian cults that worshipped fire and water. The gods of these pagan indigenous people were many, including Apas, the goddess of water, and Atar, the god of fire (Agni for the Brahmans). The Amesha (the Immortals) and Ahuras, the ethical gods, were opposed by Daevas, the evil ones, including Indra. There were many nature gods too, of the sun, earth, moon, stars, wind, and others.

Some gods were abstract, but most were anthropomorphic, including Mithra, the god of war, and Ashi, the goddess of fortune. The laws of nature, *asha* for Avestans (and *Rta* for vedic Indians), had ethical implications, and helped maintain order on earth and among men. In terms of societal values, truth, honesty, loyalty, courage, and righteousness were considered good; and falsehood and distortion of the truth were considered bad.

According to pagan traditions, importance was given to notions of purity and pollution, and the mode of worship was simple. A sacred fire was kept alight in a small container, before which sat a priest cross-legged on the ground, in the manner still seen among Zoroastrians and Hindus. The juice of the *haoma* plant (*soma* in Sanskrit) was mixed with milk as a ritual offering, along with consecrated meat. It was believed that the spirits of sacrificed animals were absorbed into a divine being who nourished man and beast on earth.

The spirits of dead humans departed to a subterranean kingdom of the dead, ruled by Yima (Yama in Sanskrit); and it was the responsibility of the descendents of the dead to feed and clothe them for the next thirty years, roughly one generation. The dead were buried, and the rituals prescribed for the first three days after death helped the spirit reach its destination. Other rituals, performed monthly for the first year and annually for the next three decades, ensured the well-being of the departed spirit.

The worthy few, such as priests, princes, warriors who

had served the gods, and commoners who had offered many sacrifices, could expect to cross the "Crossing of the Separator" bridge connecting heaven and earth, to join the gods in sunlit paradise and there enjoy unimaginable delights. This hope of attaining paradise was accompanied by a belief in resurrection of the body. Other less-worthy souls and lowly persons, including all women and children, were believed to fall off the Bridge into the dreadful kingdom of the dead.

Zoroaster's doctrine emerged from, but went far beyond, these indigenous religious beliefs of his pagan community. He was both a prophet and the chief priest of his people; and he preached a salvation faith—the first of its kind—that promised justice and peace after passing into the next world. Life and death followed each other in an unending cycle of being; and there was life for the *urvan* or disembodied spirit (soul) after death of the individual.

The rites for restoring purity after various forms of contamination required the recitation of holy words by priests in Avestan, the sacred language of the faith. Zoroaster also introduced new religious practices, including the wearing of a knotted cord around the waist, praying five times daily at prescribed times, celebrating seven main festivals annually, and sharing communal meals for the rich and poor alike. He introduced a short prayer that served as the main form of supplication, which could also take the place of all other forms of worship in times of need. The verses of the *Gatha*, the inspired hymns attributed to Zoroaster, and the new Zoroastrian creed exalted *Ahura Mazda* as the only God worthy of being worshiped.

The prophet Zoroaster thus taught a new set of doctrines, moral values, and religious practices that served to bind his followers into a distinct community, very different from the pagans around them. The initial years of his mission, when he preached to his own tribe, were very difficult, and he made little progress. But Zoroaster was soon accorded due recognition and respect by a neighboring tribe, and lived a long and fruitful life teaching God's word. By the time of his shocking assassination by an unconverted pagan priest, a new faith had firmly taken root. This was around 1500 BCE.

By the ninth century BCE, when the religion's main features were first recorded in the history of western Iran, it had become known as the religion of all the Iranian peoples. A few centuries later, the first Persian Empire—established in 549 BCE by Cyrus the Great, a loyal worshiper of Ahura Mazda—was predominantly Zoroastrian. It covered a large area, including Asia Minor and Babylon, but the Iranian king encouraged toleration of the faiths of all his subjects, including the Jews. Cyrus went so far as to allow the Jews to return from Babylonian exile to Jerusalem, to rebuild their holy Temple there. The Jews hailed Cyrus in their scriptures as a messiah who had acted in the name and with the authority of their God *Yahweh*; and they became receptive to Zoroastrian influences. Jewish beliefs included the honoring of *Yahweh* as the sole Creator—as *Ahura Mazda* had earlier been worshiped by Zoroaster.

Within mainstream Zoroastrianism, the process of assimilation of other gods continued after the passing of the prophet Zoroaster, and took several centuries, mostly the result of Persian innovations. Ishtar, the alien goddess of love and war, whose cult had previously absorbed other mother-goddesses, was included in the pantheon; and some Iranian kings invoked the divine triad of Ahura Mazda, Anahita, and Mithra. During the third century BCE, an image cult was added, and the mother-goddess was venerated as a richly-adorned statue. As a counter-measure to this unorthodox practice of venerating man-made icons, the temple worship of fire was introduced by orthodox priests—thereby giving rise to the common perception that Zoroastrians were "fire-worshipers" instead of worshipers of only the un-created God, *Ahura Mazda*.

BELIEFS AND PRACTICES

ZOROASTER WAS THIRTY years old when the first revelations came to him, after he received a vision in which a shining being led him into the presence of *Ahura Mazda* (God) and five other radiant beings. He subsequently saw Ahura Mazda a number of times in visions, or felt his presence or heard his words summoning him to service, which Zoroaster whole-heartedly obeyed. Initially, he venerated Mazda according to traditional beliefs, as the master of *asha* (order, righteousness, and justice); but then he was inspired to go much further to proclaim Ahura Mazda as the *one* uncreated God—the all-wise, wholly-just, and wholly-good transcendent Creator of all else that is good, including all other beneficent divinities.

The other divinities emanated from Ahura Mazda, but maintained the essential unity of the beneficent, in a manner similar to a torch lighting other torches. The Amesha Spentas, the divine beings, strived to do their appointed tasks, furthering good and defeating evil. The six Holy Immortals personified good purpose, righteousness, devotion, the power of the kingdom of God, moral and spiritual health, and eternal well-being in the presence of Ahura Mazda.

The Zoroastrian prophet also saw in a vision another equally-uncreated being, Angra Mainyu, who opposed Ahura Mazda and was totally-ignorant and wholly-evil. These twin primal spirits, the good and the bad, were always in conflict, just as man must continually choose between good and evil. In the end, however, Ahura Mazda, and those who choose the right actions, would prevail. Spenta Mainyu (the Holy Spirit) would help destroy all evil so that the universe would be wholly-good forever. Instead of a continuous cycle of birth and death—assuming that the gods and man did their part—human history would end in eternal perfection. Ahura Mazda, the divinities, and all men and women would then live together eternally in untroubled goodness and peace.

Being the creation of Ahura Mazda, man had a duty to seek his own moral well-being, defeating evil in whatever form it exists, and caring for the world and fellow-humans, all created by God. Zoroaster also taught that the Daevas, evil by nature and wicked by choice—like Angra Mainyu himself—were the false gods that were not to be worshipped, because they led man to greed, conflict, bloodshed, and strife.

According to Zoroaster, as each spirit departed from the earth upon death, it would be judged on what it had done during this life through ethical actions that had promoted goodness. Every soul could therefore aspire to cross the "Bridge of the Separator" if the good it had done was judged to be greater than the bad, when weighed on the scales of moral goodness. After this judgment of each individual, the soul could attain everlasting paradise where it would be reunited with its resurrected body. Those who failed this test would be forever tormented in hell, presided over by Angra Mainyu.

The final separation of the righteous from the wicked would take place at the Last Judgment. All those who had ever lived, including those who had been judged already, would have to pass through a river of molten metal, and the wicked would suffer a second death and perish forever. The Daevas and legions of darkness, as well as Angra Mainyu and all evil, would be completely annihilated. Only the good would live on eternally, in bliss.

Zoroaster was thus the first prophet in recorded history to teach about the uncreated- Creator, and the doctrines of individual judgment, heaven and hell, the future resurrection of the body, the Last Judgment, and life-everlasting for the reunited soul and body. He also taught about the unwavering impartiality of divine justice, based on the morality of an individual's own thoughts, words, and deeds. Only moral merit, not material power, mattered for man's entry into paradise. All these divinely-inspired teachings of Zoroaster were fundamentally new, and they dramatically modified indigenous polytheistic pagan beliefs.

In the centuries that followed, Zoroastrians gradually spread into Central Asia, and steadily developed their doctrine and liturgical practices. The evolving Zoroastrian pantheon of divinities had gods of the sky, sun, earth, fire, water, plants, and others, similar to the pagan traditions of the region, but now they all served Ahura Mazda.

There also developed a belief in the imminent end of the world, and the coming of a Saoshyant or Savior, born to a virgin through immaculate conception, who would rouse mankind in the final struggle against evil. Later still, in the Younger Avesta, the prophet Zoroaster himself came to be exalted, though he was never divinized.

The *Avesta*, the sacred books of Zoroastrians, include the *Gathas*, the seventeen great hymns composed by Zoroaster himself and preserved by his followers, as well as later liturgical hymns, texts, and *mantras*. The Gathas are inspired passionate poems addressed directly to God, and are based on the prophet's personal experience of the divine. Zoroaster believed he was God's messenger to all mankind, and was transmitting the revealed words of divine wisdom.

During the sixth century CE, the Avesta, which had thus far only been transmitted orally, was first written down. It used a specially-devised Avestan alphabet that modified the Persian (Pahlavi) script. By the ninth century CE, a twenty-one book canon was decreed. It contained the Gathas and its associated texts, other scholarly works and law books, and instructions for priests. Ordinary family priests and the laity continued to worship and pray with words that had been faithfully transmitted orally from one generation to the next, since the beginning of the faith. In 957 CE, parts of the Avesta were transcribed for the first time into Arabic, the language of Islam's *Holy Qur'an*.

The prophet Zoroaster's original teachings spread throughout the Near East, from Egypt to the Black Sea. In essence, the faith's fundamental doctrines included belief in the Creator (the supreme God), in an evil power that opposes him, and in many lesser divinities that help Ahura Mazda combat evil. The world had been created for a purpose, but would come to an end which would be heralded by the coming of a cosmic Savior. In the meantime, there was heaven and hell, and the human soul upon death would be individually judged. At the end of time, the dead would be resurrected for the Last Judgment, the wicked would be completely destroyed, and the kingdom of God would be established on earth. The righteous would enter into the garden of paradise, and would forever dwell happily in the presence of God, immortal themselves in body and soul.

The earlier purity laws of the Indo-Iranians were also developed further, to cover various aspects of personal cleanliness and the sanctity of the earth, animals, plants, water, and especially fire. Upon death, which was considered the greatest polluter, the naked human body was laid down on the bare ground to be devoured by scavenging birds and beasts, after which the bones bleached in the sun were gathered and buried to await Judgment Day. The disembodied soul was believed to be drawn up by the rays of the sun on the fourth day after death to face Mithra at the Chinvat Bridge.

Roots and Branches

WITH THE PASSAGE of time, parts of the Persian Empire—which was largely Zoroastrian—came under the rule of others, notably after the invasion of Asia Minor in 311 BCE by Alexander the Great. Zoroastrianism competed for attention with Greek and Roman beliefs in the west, and with Parthian ideas and to some extent Mahayana

Buddhism in the east. In due course, Aramaic was gradually replaced by Greek, Parthian, and then by Persian as the Zoroastrians' language for written communication.

The ebb and flow of power and people led to the intermingling of devotional practices, and despite periodic persecution by various rulers, the Zoroastrian faith continued to be practiced in various regions of Iran and Inner Asia for many centuries. It was only from the third century CE onwards that its geographical spread towards the west was stopped by the emergence of Christianity. Within Iran itself, the widespread practice of Zoroastrianism continued for several more centuries, until it was decisively curtailed by the rise of Islam after the seventh century CE.

During this latter period, many Zoroastrians were forcibly converted to Islam. Fearing this, in 936 CE a small group of Zoroastrians took refuge in Gujarat in western India, where they came to be known as Parsees (from Persia). But in Iran, the difficulties faced by the followers of Zoroaster continued. In the twelfth century CE, pagan Mongol invaders destroyed great collections of Zoroastrian holy books, including every copy of the Sasanian Avesta.

By the thirteenth century CE, only small pockets of Zoroastrians remained in Iran, near Yazd and Kerman. Most residents of Iran—the Zoroastrians' ancestral homeland—were by now Muslim; but the Zoroastrian faith still survived, despite all the violence it had endured for centuries. Remarkably, at the turn of the 21st century CE, two of the Zoroastrian fires still worshiped in Yazd are ancient—and have been burning continuously for over 2000 years.

Despite these efforts of the faithful, the ups and downs of history have taken a heavy toll on Zoroastrianism. The ancient religion founded by the prophet Zoroaster now has only a few million followers, mostly in India and Iran. But this decline in numbers over the past two millennia does not detract from the significant spiritual legacy of the prophet Zoroaster, the founder of one of the oldest of our living faiths—a religion with remarkable new teachings that remain the essence of Zoroastrianism. It is striking too that many of these beliefs resonate, in somewhat modified form, in the Abrahamic religions that developed in the Middle East, and can also be found in muted tones in some Indic religions of South Asia.

Chapter 3

Judaism

CREATION AND EVOLUTION

THE JEWISH PEOPLE have been especially chosen by *Yahweh* (God) to help achieve His purpose on earth. This belief of the people of Israel originated with the patriarch Abraham, who obeyed God's command to establish a new tribe/ nation. Abraham, the first Jew, was a descendent of the prophet Noah whom God had saved in the great Flood, along with a male and female of every species of animal and bird. According to Abraham's story as recounted in the "Book of Genesis" of the *Torah* (the *Hebrew Bible*), his eldest son was Ishmael, born to an Egyptian slave woman named Hagar. Ishmael later became father of all the Arab tribes. Abraham's younger son was Isaac, born to his wife Sarah when he was a hundred years old. Isaac's son Jacob—later named Israel, meaning "He who strives with God"—became father of the twelve tribes of Israel.

The early Israelites were semi-nomadic shepherds and farmers residing in the Near East since before 1300 BCE. Some members of these tribes were exiled from Canaan (Palestine) to Egypt; and were later led out of slavery to the promised holy land in Canaan by the prophet Moses, who acted in accordance with God's Will and with His direct help, through the miraculous parting of the waters of the Red Sea. God revealed his divine message to Moses on two tablets of stone that He himself had written in Hebrew. This happened on Mount Sinai in Palestine during the 13th (or perhaps the 14th) century BCE. The message conveyed by Yahweh to Moses was later recorded in the Hebrew Bible's Book of Exodus. (Exodus 9-18, 24:12, 31:18 and 32:16)

The Hebrew Bible recounts the history of the Jewish people during the fourteen or so centuries preceding the birth of Jesus of Nazareth. According to this account, King David, the second King of Israel, captured Jerusalem around 1000 BCE; and his son Solomon built the first Jewish Temple. In the 8th century BCE, the prophet Isaiah proclaimed that a descendent of King David would be born to a young maiden who would name him Immanuel, and this powerful king would rule over the Jewish people with justice and righteousness. He would seek vengeance against the enemies of Israel, and as a Messiah would bring peace and order on earth. (Isaiah 7:14)

Unfortunately, as recorded in the Hebrew Bible, this prophecy did not come to pass. The Temple built in Jerusalem by King Solomon was destroyed by the Babylonians in 586 BCE. It was rebuilt in 515 BCE after the return of the Jews from exile in Babylon. The Persian King Cyrus had allowed the Jews to return from Babylon to Jerusalem; and the second prophet Isaiah proclaimed Cyrus a "messiah" (meaning, in Hebrew, "anointed by God"). The Jewish people had high regard for the religious tolerance of King Cyrus, who was Zoroastrian; and the Jewish and Persian peoples co-existed peacefully in Babylon and its surrounding region for many centuries. Their religious beliefs and practices were fairly compatible, and they mutually-influenced each other in many ways.

The messages of God's justice and mercy conveyed by Moses and other Jewish prophets were initially composed and transmitted orally in Hebrew, the language of the Jewish people. With the passage of time, though Hebrew remained the language of the Jewish scripture (hence, the "Hebrew Bible"), Aramaic gradually became the dominant language of the people of Palestine. It was the language spoken by the preacher-prophet Jesus, who was born and died a Palestinian Jew. The Hebrew scripture had been translated into Greek, which was also the language in which Jesus's teachings and those of his closest followers were first written during the first few centuries of the Common Era.

Various prophesies and events are recorded in the Hebrew Bible, which provides both a historical and a religious narrative of the Jewish people. Jewish religious doctrine had initially been composed and transmitted orally for many centuries before it was handwritten on parchment scrolls. It was later assembled in a codex during the first century CE, and finally the texts were brought together as Scripture in book form. The Hebrew Bible, also called the *Torah*, consists of many books that were written at various times by various authors, most of them presently unknown.

The first Jewish writings probably date to the 8th to 6th centuries BCE (or possibly earlier). The writings now ascribed to prophet Moses—which constitute the first five books of the Hebrew Bible—were finalized in book form during the 2nd century BCE. The collection of canonized books that constitute this Bible were written, interpreted, edited, and assembled during the course of nine hundred years, between the 5th century BCE and the 4th century CE. They contain the revealed word of God, the inspired messages of Jewish prophets and sages, and the commentaries and interpretations of learned teachers and rabbis.

The authors and exact dates of most of these texts are not known; but the Hebrew Bible contains books ascribed to many prophets, all of whom spoke for or with divine authority. It contains messages revealed to Moses (14th century BCE), and to the "major prophets", including Isaiah (8th century BCE) and Jeremiah (6th century BCE). It also contains the messages ascribed to the twelve "minor prophets," including Hosea, Amos, Jonah, Micah, Zechariah, and others, which were written at various times, up to the 2nd century BCE or thereabouts. By this time, the canon of Judaic biblical literature was largely closed.

The first five books of Moses—titled Genesis, Exodus, Leviticus, Numbers, and Deuteronomy—are collectively known as the *Pentateuch*, sometimes also called the *Torah* or the Written Law, since these are the revealed Truth dictated personally by God to Moses on Mount Sinai. As noted earlier, most books of the Jewish Bible were originally in Hebrew, though some parts of the texts written after the Babylonian exile were in Aramaic, the language used at that time in daily life.

All these books were translated into Greek around the 3rd century BCE to make them more accessible to the Jewish people, who by then were more familiar with Greek than Hebrew. The Greek translation of the Jewish (Hebrew) Bible is known as the *Septuagint*. The Hebrew Bible, comprised of the books of Moses and of the other Jewish prophets, is also known to Christians as the "Old Testament," to distinguish it from the New Testament of the followers of Jesus Christ.

Many interpretations (*midrash*) and commentaries on the Torah were written during the 2nd to 7th centuries CE, as were new laws and judgments of Jewish scholars. Many of these were in Aramaic, the language of the region. In the 6th and 7th centuries CE, a collection of such texts was prepared, assembled, and finalized by Babylonian rabbis into a single book; and became known as the *Talmud*. This Babylonian Talmud is arguably more-highly regarded than the Talmud prepared a century or so earlier by rabbis in Jerusalem.

Beliefs and Practices

GOD REVEALED TO Moses that the Jews must henceforth worship only the one true God, and should not worship any idols or images of other gods as they had been doing till then. Accordingly, the foundational Jewish creed was proclaimed to be: "Hear, O Israel, the Lord your God is one." (Deuteronomy, 6:4).

The new message from God enabled the Jews to

recognize the grandeur of their all-powerful, all-good, and loving God—who had Chosen them as a special people, and had revealed to them His Truth. They rhetorically asked: "Who is like you among the gods, O Yahweh?" [YHWH, since ancient Hebrew had no vowels]; "What great nation has a God like the Lord?" And they sang in gratitude: "Happy are you, O Israel. Who is like you, a people saved by Yahweh?" (Deuteronomy, 33:29).

Until the coming of Moses, the Jews had been a polytheistic people, like other Mediterranean tribes that worshiped pagan gods and performed a variety of rites and rituals. They believed in anthropomorphic gods and goddesses, some of whom displayed ordinary human frailties such as anger, pride, jealousy, vengeance, and adultery. The Hebrew Bible speaks also of a number of gods related to the forces of nature. It records the Jewish practice of child- and animal sacrifice—even by some prophets—as well as sexual rites of fertility with close kin. Justice, ritual, and sacrifice were emphasized. The prophets revealed the judgments of the gods, and served religious and social functions; and the priests ensured that cultic rites were properly performed and ritual purity was maintained.

However, now that it had been revealed by God that the previous gods were not worthy of worship, the Jewish people were required to exclusively honor and worship only Yahweh. Even though Yahweh could not be directly known or understood, in the distant past He had helped the prophets Noah, Abraham, Isaac, Jacob, and others; and even now He continued to directly help Moses and the Jews—His Chosen people—in all the historical events unfolding on earth. He asked the Jewish people to observe

His commandments, and thereby help establish God's realm of justice and peace (*shalom*) on earth.

With the passage of time, the Jewish religion evolved further. The rabbis' fresh interpretations of their old religious texts, their new understandings of the laws of moral and social behavior contained therein, and the voluminous commentaries on these texts by various scholars helped form what came to be known as Rabbinic Judaism. Strictly obeying the laws of Moses as recorded in the Torah, and following the interpretations and laws proclaimed by the rabbis and priests, were considered a religious duty of all Jews. Male circumcision and abstention from pork were required as signs of loyalty to the covenant with Yahweh, but women were not expected to devote themselves to the study of religious texts.

There are 613 commandments from Yahweh in the Torah, of which 248 are positive (do's) and 365 negative (don'ts). The most important are the Ten Commandments (Deuteronomy 5:6-22, and Exodus 20:2-17) revealed to Moses on Mount Sinai, the first two of which are: "Thou shalt have none other gods before me;" and "Thou shalt not make thee any graven image, or any likeness of any thing that is in heaven above….[and] Thou shalt not bow down thyself unto them, nor serve them: for I the Lord thy God am a jealous God." Other instructions revealed in these ancient Commandments to Moses when the Lord talked with him face to face (as per the Hebrew Bible) require that Jews honor their father and mother, keep the Sabbath day, and not kill, commit adultery, steal, bear false witness, or covet their neighbor's wife or material possessions.

In the Torah and Talmud there are many other laws as

well, covering various aspects of daily living—such as what food is permitted (*kosher*) or forbidden, and how it is to be prepared, cooked, and eaten; as well as various rituals, rules of hygiene, and moral laws. Divine instructions for constructing the tabernacle or Ark for housing the Israelites' covenant with God and the two tablets of stone upon which God wrote the Ten Commandments revealed to Moses, are included as well. (Exodus 31:18, and 32:16; Deuteronomy 5:22)

Yahweh had also enabled the Jewish people to grasp spiritual realities through worship and prayer. Inspired by God's messages, the Jews developed a belief in bodily resurrection after death, and hence buried the dead body. The human body was also honored with a burial— and was not cremated—because mankind was made in God's image. Jews believed too in everlasting life for the soul in either heaven or hell, depending on how well—i.e., how morally, in accordance with the Hebrew Bible—the individual's human life had been lived on earth.

The core of Judaism is the belief in the oneness of God (Yahweh) whose Will is revealed in the Covenant with the Jewish people. This only God, the one Creator, ultimately controls the destiny of all mankind and the world. The human being is essentially good—for humans have been "made in God's image" (Genesis 1:27)—and are endowed with reason and intelligence so that they may choose between good and evil. The Torah has been revealed by God to guide this choice, but eventually all humans, Jews and non-Jews, will be judged by God, and the righteous will be rewarded and the wicked punished. Finally, the time will come when the Messiah, a descendent of the Jewish King David, will come to the earth to establish the divine kingdom of truth, righteousness, and justice.

These and other Jewish traditions evolved throughout the first millennium BCE; and by the first century CE, several competing Jewish sects and interpretations of the Hebrew texts had emerged. These included the teachings of the prophet Jesus and his followers (which later became the Christian scripture), as well as the sectarian beliefs of the Samaritans, Essenes, Pharisees, Sadducees, and others.

The beliefs of these sects differed in important ways. For example, with respect to the human spirit or soul: the Sadducees believed that the soul perishes with the body; the Essenes regarded the soul as immortal; and the Pharisees believed that while a soul is imperishable, the soul of the good passes into another body, but the soul of the wicked suffers eternal punishment. The Pharisees accepted the promise of resurrection of the human body at the end of time; but the Sadducees emphatically rejected the idea of the "life to come" and the notion of resurrection of the body.

Other differences of doctrine, belief, and practice were significant too; but after much debate, a common consensus began to emerge, and gradually received general acceptance. By the 2nd century CE, the Hebrew Bible had divisions comprising the Law, Prophets, and Writings, though final shape had yet to be given to this canon.

As noted in the New Testament of the Christians, the Jewish Temple that had been built in Jerusalem during the sixth century BCE was destroyed by the Romans in 70 CE. (Only a small section of the Temple's western wall now remains.) After this major calamity, Jewish worship shifted from the central Temple and its priests in Jerusalem to the more numerous synagogues and Jewish teachers (rabbis) who lived among the ordinary people in scattered settlements.

Most Jews did not accept the Jewish preacher Jesus as their Messiah, for he was not a descendent of King David and had not ruled over the Jewish people with peace and justice, as promised by the Jewish prophets. Jews also did not accept the (nascent Christian) belief in the virgin birth of Jesus and his divine bodily resurrection to heaven after death. The notion of paradise or general resurrection as a reward for a righteous life was not yet considered established doctrine. The foundation of the Jewish faith remained the actual ancient covenant between God and the people of Israel; and Jews firmly believed their Bible's historical accounts of how Yahweh had directly participated in the lives of the Jewish people and their prophets, and how He would continue to guide them in the future.

Because the second (Jewish) Temple had been destroyed in 70 CE and there was no central place for worship, the synagogue gained prominence as the primary sacred space and community center. From the 3rd century CE onwards, every synagogue had a set of hand-written Torah scrolls kept in a special alcove (called the *ark*) facing Jerusalem. Jews came together at the synagogue for communal prayers and services, for studying the Torah and Talmud, for celebrating religious festivals, and for various other social purposes.

During the centuries that followed, Jewish beliefs in the messages of the ancient Hebrew texts were increasingly complemented by new teachings of priests and rabbis. Justice and ethical living in accordance with God's Laws became more important than the performance of cultic rituals and animal sacrifice. Also, the evolving Jewish doctrine sought to more-clearly distinguish Judaism from the concurrently-evolving religion of Christianity. Thus was created the "Oral Torah" that supplements the "Written Torah" revealed to Moses.

Roots and Branches

THE EXTENSIVE LITERATURE of newly-inspired interpretations of the original Torah and laws for guiding the Jewish community have continued to evolve throughout the past two thousand years. Public congregational prayers still require a minimum quorum of ten adult Jewish males; and women and girls often do not take part in religious services. Women are, however, important in family life in orthodox Judaism, and having a Jewish mother is enough to make one Jewish; others can convert to Judaism through marriage. These and other Jewish traditions have continued, though with the passage of time, different sects of Judaism have emerged.

There are now an estimated thirteen million Jews in the world; and about half of these are in America. Some Jewish sects trace their origins to Europe (the Ashkenazi Jews) and the Middle East and Mediterranean region (the Sephardic Jews), where there are other Jewish sects as well. In America, there are the Orthodox, Hasidic, Reconstructionist, Reform, Conservative, Messianic, and Jewish Fundamentalist sects.

In the United States, the main Jewish sects differ, to varying extent, on doctrine and practice. For the Orthodox Jews, the Torah and traditional forms of worship and observance are paramount. Hasidic Jews are more conservative, and live in segregated communities that preserve their ancestors' way of life and worship. The Fundamentalists wish to reclaim the Land of Israel in preparation for the establishment of a messianic kingdom.

In contrast, the Reconstuctionists accept the evolution of Judaism, and seek to demonstrate that it can be practiced within modern society. Reform Judaism promotes assimilation into American culture; and Conservative Jews are willing to make changes in customs, but strive to observe the requirements of the Torah as closely as possible in a modern setting. Messianic Jews differ from all these other sects. Because they accept Yeshua (Jesus of Nazareth) as the messiah and savior, they are not recognized as "Jewish" by the other Jewish denominations.

Chapter 4

Hinduism

CREATION AND EVOLUTION

HINDUISM IS KNOWN as the *sanatana dharma* (ancient religion, or the Eternal Truth). It does not have an identifiable founder or date of creation—though it is known that during the second millennium BCE, it introduced inspired beliefs and practices into indigenous religious traditions of northern India.

The Aryans from Central Asia brought with them ancient knowledge (*Veda*, in Sanskrit) that provided the foundation for hymns of the *Rg Veda*, the earliest-known scripture of the people later known as Hindus who lived around the Sindhu river. These polytheistic groups worshiped many deities and nature gods, including *Brahman,* who initially signified "sacred knowledge." Later, Brahman came to be identified with the entire universe, as the One God, the Creator, or Supreme Being.

"In the beginning, this universe was Being only, one only, without a second." "This whole universe is Brahman." (*Chandogya Upanishad*, IV.ii; III.xiv).

Brahman, the Creator, is both *saguna* (with attributes) and *nirguna* (without attributes). God's Spirit (spiritual energy) sustains the whole universe and is present in all things. But since God is infinite, He cannot be comprehended by finite human beings or described in any way except as "*neti, neti*" ("not this, not this"). The chief attributes of Brahman are "*sat, chit, ananda*," meaning that God is "Pure Being, Awareness, and Bliss." *Maya* is the power of Brahman to make things manifest; and the whole world is His *lila* (God's play). Brahmanic religious tradition also emphasizes worship of other cosmic beings and spirits, as well as ritualistic animal sacrifice to propitiate various gods.

Brahmanic hymns, *mantras*, and chants of the Rg Veda give an idea of Hinduism during this formative period. Its oldest hymns were composed around 1400 BCE. The largest number of hymns in the Rg Veda (one-fourth of the 1028 hymns) honor Indra, the creator god, who created the sun, dawn, and all other things. The ancient Brahmanic pantheon had many other gods too, some with anthropomorphic features. Most were nature gods, such as *Agni* (the god of sacrificial fire, the most prominent deity after Indra), Rudra (the wielder of the thunder-bolt), Vishnu (associated with the sun), Vayu (wind), Usas (dawn), Parjanya (rain), and Varuna (water and oceans). Vedic Hindus also worshiped many other deities (and demons) and nature, including the deity Soma (an intoxicating plant juice used in sacrificial rituals), and India's main rivers (which were worshiped as goddesses).

The creation myths of the Rg Veda connected Hinduism to the beginning of the universe. A hymn from its tenth book says that the entire universe emerged from the sacrifice of a primordial cosmic Being called *Purusha* ("the Man"). According to the Rg Veda: "From his mind the moon was born, and from his eye the sun, from his mouth Indra and the fire [Agni], and from his breath the wind [Vayu] was born. From his navel arose the atmosphere, from his head the sky evolved, from his feet the earth, and from his ear the cardinal points of the compass: so did they [the deities who performed the sacrifice] fashion forth these worlds." (*Rg Veda*, X, xc: 13-14)

The primary social groups comprising ancient Vedic society arose from this primal sacrifice too. "The brahman [*brahmin*] was His [Purusha's] mouth, the arms were made the prince [the warrior, *kshatriya*], his thighs the common people [*vaishya*], and from his feet the serf [*shudra*] was born." (*Rg Veda*, X, xc: 12). The four main Hindu castes thus have a cosmic Vedic origin, as revealed in the Rg Veda.

Besides the *Rg Veda*—which contains laudatory hymns, mantras, and prayers to the deities—there are three other Vedas. These are the *Yajur Veda*, which gives detailed rules and procedures for performing rituals and sacrifices; the *Sama Veda*, which focuses on sacred chants; and the *Atharva Veda*, whose hymns are magical spells and incantations that originated in about 900 BCE. Inspired sages initially vocalized the Vedas, which were then preserved and transmitted by Brahmin priests for many centuries before being compiled into written sacred texts.

The oldest, the *Rg Veda*, was written in Sanskrit during the second millennium BCE, probably around 1200 BCE. After this came the other three Vedas; then the *Puranas* (ancient mythological history), which are stories of the creation and lives of gods; and then books of religious speculation that later led to philosophical works. These took their final form during the period 700-300 BCE, more than 1000 years after the Vedas.

There are eighteen Puranas, mostly mythological epics describing the powers and exploits of Lord Vishnu and Lord Shiva and their incarnations. Of these, the *Bhagavad Purana* and the *Ramayana* are famous for the stories they tell of the lives respectively of Lord Krishna and Lord Rama. The final version of the Ramayana was perhaps completed about two thousand years ago. The *Brahmanas*, composed between 800 BCE and 500 BCE are ritual instructions; and the *Arayanakas* ("forest books") are reflections on the meanings of rituals.

During the period 800 BCE to 200 BCE came the *Upanishads,* which embody a shift from sacrificial rituals towards more personalized worship and metaphysical speculation. The Upanishads introduced new insights on reincarnation, thereby supplementing Vedic rituals (for obtaining rewards in this life) with beliefs and practices that focus on the next life. The teachings of the Upanishads also help mankind achieve liberation (*moksha*) from the endless cycle of rebirth.

Hindus believe that the ancient holy words of the Vedas have always existed, and were first communicated to sages and seers around 1400 BCE-1200 BCE. The Vedas were revealed to the sages rather than composed by them; and hence are known as *sruti* (that which is heard). Other sacred texts, written during the course of the subsequent fifteen hundred years, are considered *smriti* (the remembered text). From the orthodox perspective, the smriti texts (which are numerous, and were written over many centuries) are considered authoritative only to the extent that they do not contradict the sruti texts, the original Vedic scripture.

After the Vedas, the best known religious texts are the *Mahabharata*, the *Bhagavad Gita*, and the *Ramayana*. The Mahabharata is an account of the descendents of the house of Bharata (India is now known as Bharat). It is the longest mythological poem ever composed anywhere in the world; and its 90,000 couplets are together about seven times the length of the *Illiad* and *Odyssey* combined. Its authorship is traditionally attributed to the poet Vyasa, who probably lived around 500 BCE.

It was during this period, between 800 BCE and 500 BCE, that the polytheism of the Vedas gradually gave way to monotheism, a moral code emerged, and the main features of Hinduism were established. By teaching that there is only One God (*Brahman*) who takes many forms (*avatars*), the new sacred texts reinterpreted the Vedas, but maintained its underlying unity in diversity.

One part of the Mahabharata is the epic poem known as the Bhagavad Gita (Song of the Lord). In the *Gita*, Lord Krishna (as charioteer) explains to the noble warrior Arjuna the duties of Hindu *dharma*, the importance of loving devotion (*bhakti*) of God, and the moral principles that ought to govern relationships among humans. The setting is a momentous battle between two princely clans on the plains of Panipat (north of Delhi) during the last half of the first millennium BCE. However, though the Gita is essentially a dialogue between Lord Krishna and Arjuna, its message is universal, and is meant for all mankind.

In the Bhagavad Gita, Lord Krishna tells Arjuna that he should not hesitate to do battle—for killing only slays the body, while the soul is indestructible. "Never is he born nor dies; never did he come to be, nor will he ever come to be again; Unborn, eternal, everlasting is he—primeval; He is not slain when the body is slain." (Gita, II.20). Also, says Krishna: "The four-caste system did I generate" (Gita, IV.13); and it is Arjuna's religious duty (*svadharma*) as a *kshatriya* to fight with complete disregard for the fruits of his actions. Lord Krishna teaches also that each person should perform only the duties of his own caste (*varna*). "Do the work that is prescribed for thee." (Gita, III.8) "Better to do one's [caste] duty, though devoid of merit, than to do another's, however well performed. By doing the works prescribed by his own nature, a man meets with no defilement." (Gita, XVIII.41)

Similarly, the Ramayana, which is a sacred epic story of the life of Lord Rama—who ruled in Ayodhya in northern India around 1500 BCE—conveys deeper messages that are at the heart of the Hindu faith. It was composed in Sanskrit by the poet Valmiki sometime between 200 BCE and 200 CE. Both the Bhagavad Gita and the Ramayana illustrate what it means to be a good Hindu in all aspects of life. Adherence to their teachings in thought and deed enables accumulation of good *karma*, which leads to the eventual attainment of *moksha* in this or subsequent lives.

A prayer from the Upanishads voices the Hindu's primary goal: he seeks divine help for moving from the unreal to the real, from darkness to light, from death to immortality. The Bhagavad Gita instructs how this goal can be achieved. It says that those who worship the infinite, the transcendent unmanifested, who have all the powers of their soul in harmony, and who find joy in the good of all beings, reach in truth the Supreme Being's very Self.

The detailed rules to be followed during daily life were prescribed in the sacred texts as well. The most extensive and best-known legal text of ancient India was written by the sage Manu around 200 CE, and is known as the *Law Code of Manu*. It includes the codes of conduct and do's and don'ts for various Hindu caste groups and occupations. In addition, it has detailed norms and penalties regarding inter-personal relationships, marriage, sexual relations, theft, etc.; and it describes various sources of food-, physical-, and other pollution. The Law Code of Manu also covers the organization of the state and judicial system; describes a variety of penalties and penances; provides insights regarding the workings of karma and reincarnation; and includes many other topics relevant for the efficacious practice of Hinduism.

Beliefs and Practices

As already noted, Hinduism believes in the One God, *Brahman*. This ultimate Supreme Reality is Transcendent outside the created world, as well as Immanent within it. Hindus believe also in incarnations of God (*avatars,* manifestations of the divine) who periodically come to this world in human and non-human form to help us understand the true nature of reality, and to free us from illusions about this world. Hindus worship many deities, gods, and goddesses, as well as rivers, mountains, and other places that are considered holy.

Hinduism believes that for creating and maintaining the material world, the Supreme God (*Brahman*) incarnates in three main forms. The Trinity (*Trimurti*) is comprised of Lord Brahma (the creator), Lord Vishnu (the preserver), and Lord Shiva (the destroyer). Members of the Trinity incarnate too, as do their manifestations. "Whenever the law of righteousness (*dharma*) withers away, and lawlessness (*adharma*) raised its head, then do I generate Myself [on earth]." (Gita, IV.7)

The ten avatars of Lord Vishnu include Lord Rama and Lord Krishna (respectively the seventh and eighth incarnations of Lord Vishnu) and the Buddha (the ninth incarnation). Invariably, the gods are married. The consort of Lord Vishnu is Lakshmi, the goddess of fortune, who is manifested as Sita (with Lord Rama) and as Radha (with Lord Krishna). Lord Shiva incarnates as Nataraja (Lord of the Dance), and in many other forms; and his consorts include the goddesses Durga, Kali, and Parvati, whose sons are Lord Ganesh (Remover of Obstacles) and Lord Kartikeyya.

Hindus believe too in the unending cycle of birth, suffering, death, and rebirth (*samsara*); and in the moral law of *karma*, according to which all thoughts and actions have consequences in the present or future lives ("you reap what you sow"). We live in a moral universe in which every human decision has antecedents in this or past lives, as well as consequences in this life and the next. But all decisions are freely arrived at, for man is a moral being and has choice.

Upon death of the body, the soul (*jiva, atman*, the Spirit within), which is the unchanging essence of every living being, reincarnates or transmigrates into human or non-human form. "For sure is the death of all that comes to birth, sure the birth of all that dies." (Gita, II.27). "As a man casts off his worn-out clothes, and takes on other new ones [in their place], so does the embodied soul cast off his worn-out bodies, and enters others new." (Gita, II.22).

The reincarnated soul continues through the endless cycle of rebirth until the negative effects of the accumulated bad karma have been worked through. The individual attains *moksha* with the realization that his soul (*atman*) is not separate from the Universal Atman (*Paramatman*). As taught in the Chandogya Upanishad, "*Tat tvam asi*" ("That (*Brahman*) thou (*atman*) art"). The individual soul then unites with Brahman and achieves moksha, which is the ultimate goal of all human beings. "He, his body left behind, is never born again; he comes to Me." (Gita, IV.9).

According to Hinduism, since God's infinite love is not a myth, all souls are ultimately saved. They continue to reincarnate until they achieve moksha or union with God. Also, since God is everywhere, there is no place like hell (where God is not present), to which a soul is damned for ever.

The four desirable goals of life are performing one's

duty or engaging in appropriate behavior (*dharma*), legitimate worldly success (*artha*), pleasure (*kama*), and liberation (*moksha*) from the cycle of rebirth, which is the ultimate goal. The four stages (*ashramas*) traditionally considered appropriate are that of a student, preparing for future roles in life (*brahmacharya*); householder, taking care of family and community (*grihastha*); retiree, engaged in reflection (*vanaprastha*); and inner-directed renouncer, unmindful of external attachments (*sannyasin*). These goals and stages are applicable to all Hindus, irrespective of their caste.

According to the Rg Veda and the Bhagavad Gita, the four Hindu castes (*varnas*) are divinely-ordained, everyone is born into and can never leave his/her caste, and each caste has a dharma (duty) appropriate to it. "The Blessed Lord said: to brahmins, princes, artisans, and serfs, works have been variously assigned by these constituents, and they arise from the nature of things as they are (*svabhava*)." (Gita, XVIII.41). "By [doing] the work that is proper to him [and] rejoicing [in the doing], a man succeeds, perfects himself." (Gita, XVIII.45). "Never should a man give up the works to which he's born." (Gita, XVIII.48)

The four main castes are the priests and seers (*brahmins*), who have an intuitive grasp of what matters most in life; warriors and administrators (*kshatriyas*), who can organize, manage, and lead others; traders, farmers, producers, and others who can work with material things (*vaishyas*); and menials, servants, and hired hands who are good at following others (*shudras*). There are many sub-castes too, each associated with a different occupation group. In addition, there are the untouchables (*outcastes*), who are on the lowest rung of the social hierarchy, have few rights, and are expected to restrict themselves to activities that cause ritual pollution, such as handling dead bodies of humans and animals.

Four religious paths (*yogas, margas*) are available for pursuing moksha. The more popular paths to moksha are devotion (*bhakti*) and action (*karma*). *Bhakti yoga* involves devotional worship of one or more personal gods or goddesses, such as Shiva, Vishnu, Krishna, Rama, Durga, Devi, or any of the other Hindu deities. It enables the devotee to personally experience the love of God, rather than merely sense the impersonal Universal force or Spirit (Brahman).

Karma yoga involves the performance of good deeds to accumulate positive *karma*; and is suited to those who wish to serve as instruments of God's Will. The Bhagavad Gita encourages dispassionate action, unmindful of its fruits, for such actions reap rewards that do not bind humans to rebirth. "Do works for Me, make Me thy highest goal, be loyal in love (bhakta) to Me, cast off [all other] attachments, have no hatred for any being at all, for all who do thus shall come to Me." (Gita, XI.55)

One can also follow the path of *jnana yoga*, seeking knowledge or insight by reflecting on and discerning the truth in Hindu philosophy and directly experiencing the Self. Or one can undertake *raja yoga*, the practice of deep meditation and concentration that requires spiritual discipline involving the body, heart, and mind. Everyone can choose the path or combination of paths that suit his/ her personal preference and stage of life.

For those following the path of knowledge, there are

various philosophical systems to choose from. The non-dualistic (*advaitya*) philosophy considers the Creator and all of His creation as one; so the Brahman and the "self" are indistinguishable ("That thou art"). The dualistic (*dvaitya*) philosophy considers Brahman and His various forms (avatars) as separate from the individual human being. Such a God can be worshiped with love and devotion. The ultimate goal of bhakti is eternal union with God (*Ishvara* or *Bhagavan*), through the deity or deities that are the object of personal devotion.

For Hindus, worship (*puja*) in the temple or at home usually involves a combination of prayer (*mantras*, chants), petition, supplication, ritualistic offerings (*prasad*), and reverential sighting (*darshan*) of the image (*murti*) of the chosen deity. A Brahmin priest is vital to worship in a temple, for he alone can enter the inner sanctuary and make offerings to the deity on behalf of the devotee. There are auspicious times and sacred places too.

Religious festivals honor and celebrate the gods with music, dance, elaborate processions, and pilgrimages to sacred rivers, mountains, lakes, and other places associated with the lives of the gods (avatars). Some of the prominent festivals are Diwali (the festival of lights, honoring Lord Rama and his consort Sita), Dusserah (to celebrate the triumph of good over evil, in honor of Lord Rama or Goddess Durga), Shivaratri (honoring Lord Shiva), Janamastami (birthday of Lord Krishna), Ganesh Chaturthi (birthday of Lord Ganesha), and Holi (the festival of color, to celebrate the New Year).

Roots and Branches

Over the course of the past three millennia, Hinduism's fundamental belief in the all-embracing, all-knowing, all-powerful, omnipresent Brahman (the Creator, the One God) has not changed. The religion still considers its Vedic and other scriptures, and the philosophical systems they propound, central to its beliefs.

The Hindu value system embraces knowledge and selfless work; emphasizes sacrifice and service to others; and considers meditation, contemplation, and renunciation appropriate means for facilitating progress towards release from the cycle of rebirth. Also valued are duty (dharma) in accordance with one's caste; engaging in worldly activities suitable for one's stage of life and temperament; and treating others with love, respect, honesty, and kindness.

So basic are these teachings that Hinduism is sometimes referred to as *varna-ashrama-dharma* (translated as "religious duty based on caste and stage of life"). Hindu religion and culture thus go together, secular and religious aspects are intertwined, and faith is integral to daily life.

However, Hinduism has also evolved significantly over the centuries. It is a growing tradition, not a fixed revelation or doctrine. In keeping with the Vedic belief that there are many ways of reaching God, diversity of belief and practice is to be expected within Hinduism. There is a choice of gods to worship; and choice too of how this is to be done. Brahman (the Supreme Being) welcomes all those who follow any of the many paths available to Hindus—for according to the Vedas, Truth is one, though sages call it by different names.

Nevertheless, and importantly, only a few of the original Vedic gods are worshiped today—mainly Indra, the weather god, and Agni, god of the sacred fire. Other Vedic gods have been transformed from nature deities to anthropomorphic gods that have immense power over human affairs as well as natural phenomena. New gods (avatars) have been added as well. Two of the gods not prominent in the Vedas are now the central deities of Hinduism. Rudra, a minor storm deity in the Rg Veda, is now known as Lord Shiva (the destroyer); and Lord Vishnu (the preserver), was a minor solar deity during Vedic times, according to the Rg Veda.

The evolution of Lord Shiva through the ages is particularly noteworthy. For inhabitants of the Indus Valley civilization during pre-Vedic times, he was Pasupati, Lord of the Animals. In the Vedas, he was Rudra, the storm god. Later, he was connected with phallic worship; and then with yoga, as Yogeswara. Now, Lord Shiva is also known as Nataraja, the Lord of the cosmic dance; and is associated with the creation and destruction of the entire universe. Similarly, Lord Vishnu has evolved from an unacceptable non-Aryan god to the position of the Supreme God, with ten incarnations, including Lord Rama, Lord Krishna, and the Buddha.

Lord Shiva and Lord Vishnu are now members of the divine Trinity, along with Lord Brahma, whose prominence has declined over time. The Lords Shiva and Vishnu have given rise to two major branches of Hinduism, known respectively as the Saivas and Vaishnavas, each with hundreds of millions of devotees. The mother

Goddess—in the form of Devi, Shakti, Saraswati, Kali, and Durga—is now more prominent than Lord Brahma. Kali was previously a non-Aryan goddess, but has gradually been identified with the supreme Godhead. The same kind of transformation has occurred in the case of Lord Krishna.

Thus, in Hinduism there are many ways of reaching God; and each god or goddess has a large following. Besides the Saivas and Vaishnavas, there are many other branches (sects and sub-sects) of Hinduism—such as the Naths, Yogis, Sants, Bhaktas, Siddhacharyas, Tantrics, and others. These sects were formed many centuries ago; but this was not the end of the story, for Hinduism has continued to evolve since then.

For example, reform or revivalist movements during just the past one thousand years have led to new sub-groups within Hinduism. Some of these are quite progressive, while others have gone back to their Vedic roots. Prominent leaders of these sects include Ramanuja (11th century CE), Ramananda (1370-1440 CE), Kabir (15th century CE), Raja Rammohan Roy (1774-1833 CE), Swami Dayanand Saraswati (1824-1883 CE), Ramakrishna Paramahamsa (1834-1886 CE), and Swami Vivekananda (1862-1902 CE).

Most sects of Hinduism recognize the primacy of the Vedas; but some recognize additional sectarian scriptures as well. The ancient sacred texts, originally written in Sanskrit—the language especially dedicated to Hindu religious discourse, and familiar only to Brahmin priests—have been translated into other Indian languages. New discourses, and commentaries on earlier texts and commentaries, have proliferated. It is virtually impossible to keep track of all the Hindu sacred texts that now exist.

During the past two millennia, norms of acceptable social and religious conduct have changed significantly as well. The ancient law codes are now ancient history. However, many religious practices still bear the imprint of rites and rituals of the distant past. In caste interactions particularly, some antiquated attitudes continue unabated, though in modified form.

Both continuity and change have thus shaped the Hindu way of life. From the beginning, Hinduism has been a religion with abundant choice; and the trend toward internal diversity has continued through the centuries. Different schools of religious thought have emerged. Monism, dualism, monotheism, polytheism, and pantheism are all to be found within the great diversity of beliefs and practices that is Hinduism.

For example, the idea that God incarnates in human form is not obvious in the Vedas and Upanishads—but the Mahabharata, Bhagavad Gita, and Ramayana are based largely on the teachings of God's incarnations. Image worship, now widely practiced, is a non-Vedic idea. The Samkhya philosophy rejects the idea of a personal God; but the bhakti movement is based on devotion to a personal deity. In contrast to both of these, the Samkara and Advaita schools reject the notion that anything other than God exists, for He alone is real, and the world is simply an illusion (*maya*).

There is a choice too of paths to salvation, philosophical systems to develop spiritual knowledge (there are six such systems), and rituals to worship the chosen avatars and God (Brahman). No one Savior or redeemer, or prophet or sage, or special form of worship, is considered absolutely- and universally necessary. There are many paths to the same goal; and a practicing Hindu can seek assistance from any number of gods, guides, and gurus. Each religious teacher or follower can choose the aspects of Hinduism that he/she considers most efficacious. The personal preference of the devotee determines which particular path he/she wishes to follow.

As in other religions, both conduct and beliefs matter—though some scholars consider correct conduct more important than creed in Hinduism. However, there are many ways of being correct, both in conduct and belief. Hinduism is thus a very diverse and complex religion. It is more a "way of life" and set of practices and rituals than a faith based on firmly-established and universally-accepted beliefs or doctrine.

Chapter 5

Jainism

THE JAIN RELIGION traces its roots to twenty-four great spiritual teachers or victors (*Jinas*) or "Ford-builders" (*Tirthankaras*) who help mankind across the river of rebirth (*samsara*) to the shore of spiritual liberation (*moksha*) from the eternal cycle of reincarnation.

The last (most recent) Jina was Mahavira Jain, whose family name was Vardhamana Jnatrputra, and who lived in northeastern India from 599-527 BCE, though some traditions say he was born in 540 BCE. He was thus a contemporary or near-contemporary of Siddhartha Gautama, the Buddha. Both preached in the same part of India at roughly the same time; and were critical of Vedic scriptures and practices, though they both shared with Hinduism the belief in *karma* (the moral law of cause and effect) and *samsara* (reincarnation). Significantly, the

Buddha and his followers are mentioned in the earliest Jain texts; just as Mahavira and the Jains are mentioned in the earliest Buddhist scriptures, the *Tipitaka*.

When Vardhamana was about thirty years old, he renounced the world and became a wandering ascetic. After twelve years of severe penance, austerities, and meditation on the nature of the self, he achieved omniscience (*kevalajnana*). The Mahavira (Great Hero) had conquered his inner feelings of selfishness, greed, and hate; and had gained the highest knowledge and insight— thus spiritually attaining the level of a Tirthankara (Jina). He was now able to continue an ancient tradition of recalling and propagating truths that already existed.

Mahavira Jain's first disciples were eleven Hindu Brahmins who debated him and were converted to Jainism by his wisdom and explanation of the Hindu *Vedas*. Mahavira taught and led his Jain followers for thirty years, and died in deep meditation at age seventy-two. Upon his demise he achieved *moksha*. His soul (*jiva*) had been cleansed of the *karma* (entanglement of the soul/spirit in material existence) accumulated from previous lives, and his pure (non-material) spirit had been released from the cycle of rebirth (reincarnation). His liberated soul (*siddha*) had now ascended to the apex of the spiritual universe, and there enjoyed complete freedom.

For the next one thousand years, Jainism co-existed peacefully in India with Buddhism and Hinduism. Jainism and Buddhism—both founded in the 6th century BCE in northern India—shared some features, interacted continually with each other, and offered an approach different from Hinduism, the other great religion of the subcontinent. By the 5th century CE, the Jains had become influential in India.

By the 13th century CE, however, with the resurgence of Hinduism and the introduction of Islam into India, Jainism went into decline, as did Buddhism. The Jain religion, unlike Buddhism, had not spread beyond India, in part because the Jain ascetics' belief in non-violence made it hard for them to undertake travel over long distances. Since its inception, Jainism has remained a minority religion in comparison with Buddhism and Hinduism, each of which has dominated the religious scene in India at different times.

There are presently about five million Jains, mostly in India. Roughly eighty percent belong to the Svetambara branch of Jainism. A vast majority of Jains are laypersons who adhere, to varying extent, to the principles and practices of the faith. For Jains, their minority status has sometimes been problematic—for Hindus have periodically sought to embrace Jainism as a sect of Hinduism, rather than accept it as a separate and distinct religion. Nevertheless, the religion founded over twenty-five hundred years ago remains vibrant, and is seeking a gradual comeback in India and abroad.

BELIEFS AND PRACTICES

JAINS RELY ONLY on the Tirthankaras, and not on any God or divine beings (gods) that help mankind. The very first mantra of Jain worship is: "I bow to the Jinas. I bow to the souls that have obtained release. I bow to the leaders of the Jain orders. I bow to the preceptors. I bow to all the Jain monks in the world."

In Jainism, *karma* is believed to actually be a form of subtle matter that adheres to the soul as it transmigrates from one life to another (this is thus different from the moral law of *karma* in Hinduism). To remove the "spiritual residue" accumulated on his/her soul from wrong actions done in previous lives, every human being needs to perform good deeds that cleanse the soul of bad karma, thus allowing it to transcend the world and attain complete freedom (*moksha*) from karmic determination and rebirth.

Jain teachings specify what actions lead to good karma, and what actions accumulate bad karma. Non-violence and asceticism are highly valued. Renunciation (*sannyasa*)—which is a more radical version of asceticism and self-denial—requires giving up one's social identity and family and other obligations, and is sometimes practiced. Jains firmly believe in the principle of non-injury (*ahimsa*) to all sentient beings; and hence are strict vegetarians. These key beliefs help overcome the evil, ignorance, and suffering that are endemic in this world.

The five Great Vows (*Mahavratas*) expected of ascetic monks are: (i) non-violence (*ahimsa*), avoiding harm to all living beings, or absence even of desire to do harm in thought, word, or deed; (ii) truthfulness (*satya*) and compassion, meaning not saying or doing anything that causes pain to others, including through tactlessness or selfishness; (iii) non-stealing (*asteya*), by avoiding greed and exploitation of others; (iv) chastity (*brahmacharya*), requiring celibacy by monks and nuns; and (v) non-attachment (*aparagriha*) to persons, places, and material things, since all worldly pleasures of daily life are transitory and illusionary, and needlessly distract one from actions that produce good karma and spiritual progress.

Laypersons not seeking to become monks or nuns are expected to take simpler vows that apply the Great Vows to worldly existence. They are expected to be vegetarian, truthful, engage only in work that does not deliberately destroy life, monogamous and faithful, reduce unnecessary attachment to material things, and behave ethically. Another key principle is non-absolutism (*anekantavada*), emphasizing the equality of all living beings. These principles are meant to be applied pragmatically and with reasonable flexibility, so long as a particular follower of Jainism is doing his/her best in the circumstances that prevail.

This essence of Jainism is based on the teachings of Mahavira and other Tirthankaras. Because of the belief in rebirth of the soul, all that is expected within each lifetime is to make some progress toward spiritual growth, on the path toward ultimately achieving moksha. To guide this process, there are many sacred texts that record the teachings of Mahavira Jain. An important text is the *Tattavarthasutra*, which details a fourteen-stage path to spiritual liberation, and is followed by all monks and nuns.

The earliest texts were written in Ardha-Magadhi, a specialized Prakrit dialect used by Jain initiates; and not in Sanskrit, the ancient sacred language of the Hindu *Vedas*, which was primarily used by Brahmin priests for Vedic ceremonies. The oldest Jain scriptures, written in the third or second century BCE (i.e., more than 300 years after Mahavira), contain the teachings of the 23rd and 24th Tirthankaras. Some of the later texts were written in Sanskrit, which by then had become a language of religious scholarship.

There are 14 *Puravas* (the Old Texts) that include teachings on the cosmos, bondage of the soul by matter, astrology, astronomy, yoga, and occult powers. Other important texts include the *Angas*, *Upangas*, *Chedasutras*, *Prakirnasutras*, *Culikasutras*, *Satkhandagama*, *Kalpasutra*, and *Bhagavatisutra*. These texts provide lessons on ethics, history, cosmology, and rules of ascetic conduct. The latter emphasize duties of monks, and observance of the essential Jain principle of non-violence (ahimsa).

Since the Tirthankaras have already been liberated from the material world, they are not expected to intercede directly in human affairs. But they do provide a reminder of the qualities that lead to spiritual transformation, and of the path that needs to be followed for achievement of release from the cycle of rebirth. The opportunity to reflect on their teachings and be inspired by their example helps instill a desire to emulate them, using the Jain sacred texts as guide.

Pious Jains of the past are also venerated, including Lord Bahubali and the Mother Goddess Ambika, among others. But despite such seeming similarities with Hinduism, there are many differences. In Jainism, time itself is beginning-less and endless; and it is the soul in its pure state (the *paramatman*) that is divine. There is no concept of a "Creator God" (*Brahman*, as in Hinduism); and Jains do not accord divine status to any of the Hindu Gods and avatars. Also, they do not accept the scriptural authority of the Vedas or other Hindu scriptures; and they deny the efficacy of sacrifices.

In Jainism, there is no reliance on a Supreme Being (God) for attaining salvation; nor a belief in a super-Soul (*Paramatman*) of which other individual souls are a part. The Vedic fire and the fire-god (*Agni*) and other deities are not ritually offered sacrifice; rituals and idol worship are not central to the faith; and sacred rivers, Vedic chants, or other Hindu practices are not believed to be purifying.

Instead, the focus of Jainism is on the spiritual path of meditation and "inner cleanliness" through the "right" faith, knowledge, and conduct in accordance with the ancient teachings of the great Tirthankaras, especially Mahavira Jain, and the sages and texts (notably the *Tattvarthasutra*) inspired by them. In accordance with their ancient creed, Jains bow only to the Tirthankaras, those who have attained moksha, the leaders and teachers of Jain orders, and all Jain monks.

Building upon its foundational beliefs, the Jain religion has evolved over time. Initially, images, idols, and temples were not considered important in Jainism; but by the second century BCE, a devotional cult had developed, centered on worship of the Tirthankaras in temples and homes. Jain temples are now similar to and sometimes more elaborate than Hindu temples, and have statues (*murtis*) or images of Mahavira and other Tirthankaras in the inner sanctum. They are a place for assembly, meditation, prayer, preaching, pilgrimage, and devotional worship (*bhakti*).

Such worship of Mahavira and other *Jinas* (Spiritual Victors, Tirthankaras) treats them as gods. As in Hinduism, it involves the intoning of *mantras* (chants), *darshan* (visual sighting) of the image of the Tirthankara, and other rituals such as anointing and decorating the image of the deity, and respectfully pouring milk, yogurt, or sandalwood water over it.

Roots and Branches

Mahavira had established mutually-dependent ascetic and lay communities of Jain followers; and with royal patronage, these groups grew in size and geographical coverage. By the 2nd century CE, however—and possibly earlier, within two centuries after the life of Mahavira—two main branches had evolved. These were the Digambara (sky clad) Jain sect, whose monks (*sadhus*) wear no clothes; and the Svetambara (white clad) sect, which is open to both monks and nuns (*sadhvis*). Both these sects, and their beliefs and practices, are based on ancient Jain scriptures considered authentic by their respective followers.

The Digambaras follow the personal example of Mahavira Jain, who believed that all possessions, including clothing, hinder liberation. Since Digambara nuns, unlike the monks, are obliged to wear clothes, they must be reborn as men before they can attain liberation. The Svetambara sect follows the *Kalpasutra*, the Book of Ritual, as well. Written in the second or first century BCE, it has the earliest known account of the life of Mahavira Jain, the twenty-fourth and final Tirthankara during the current cycle of time.

The Kalpasutra places Mahavira in relation to the Tirthankaras who preceded him. It says that the twenty-third Tirthankara, named Parsva, lived around 900 BCE (about 250 years before Mahavira); and Rishabha, the first Tirthankara, lived several million years ago, thus tracing the roots of Jainism to very ancient times indeed. (A Rishabha is mentioned in the Rg Veda too, referring to Lord Shiva, possibly reflecting common pre-Vedic cultural sources). Svetambara Jains believe that women are as capable as men of attaining moksha; and that the nineteenth Tirthankara was a woman named Mallinatha.

Many Svetambara texts are considered inauthentic by the Digambara Jains, especially those that they consider incompatible with their own interpretation of Jain doctrine regarding ascetic practice and the nature of an enlightened being, including the marvelous events associated with Mahavira's birth and renunciation. Though much of their teachings on other matters are similar, their differences on the necessity of nudity for achieving moksha and on other aspects of asceticism preached by Mahavira have remained unresolved for two millennia. The two major Jain sects have also maintained their own distinctive collections of texts that they consider scripture.

With time, a variety of sub-sects with different beliefs and practices have developed as well. The main Svetambara sub-sects are the Murtipujakas, Sthanakavasis, and Terapanthis; while the main Digambara sub-sects are the Bisapanthis and Terapanthis. Not all Jains believe in image worship (*murti puja*); and two important Svetambara sub-sects reject temples and idols altogether, concentrating instead on devotion to senior monks and the teachings of Mahavira that they embody and transmit. Some developments after the 17th century CE have emphasized direct experience over traditional doctrine, or suggest a new interpretation of non-violence ("intellectual ahimsa") that requires a non-absolutist religious attitude of universal tolerance similar to that proposed by some non-sectarian modern Hindu philosophers.

Going beyond Mahavira Jain's original teachings, some Svetambara sub-sects emphasize devotional practices, including chanting of sacred verses (mantras), meditation, worship of statues, or mysticism that seeks direct experience or realization of the ultimate reality. These devotees decorate their temples with carvings or beautiful images of the Jain pantheon—including Lakshmi, the Hindu goddess of wealth, who receives special reverence from Jains, many of whom are traders engaged in mercantile occupations that do not involve violence toward living beings.

Thus, in sum, the overall trend within Jainism since the time of Mahavira 2500 years ago has been toward increased diversity. The ancient division into Digambara and Svetambara branches was mainly due to doctrinal differences. But within these major sects, the subsequent formation of sub-sects has been due to the introduction of differences in religious practices—while maintaining an underlying unity of the Jain world-view and common belief system.

Chapter 6

Buddhism

CREATION AND EVOLUTION

SIDDHARTHA GAUTAMA ACHIEVED enlightenment—and
thus became *the Buddha*, the Enlightened- or Awakened
One—in 528 BCE in Bodh Gaya in northeastern India. He
was born in 563 BCE into a royal family, and died in 483
BCE after forty-five years of teaching the path to *nirvana*.
This state of blissful "no-self" signifies the end of desire
and attachment, release from the consequences of the
moral law of *karma*, and liberation from the unending
cycle of death and rebirth or "wandering" (*samsara*).

The Buddha's enlightenment had not come easily. It
was the result of much meditation and experimentation
with the self. Prior to his "awakening," six arduous years
of strict yoga and asceticism had come to naught, even for
one as gifted and persistent as Gautama. Neither extreme
austerity as a yogi and mendicant, nor his previous

princely-life of limitless luxury had proved beneficial, so the middle-aged Siddhartha Gautama (he was thirty-five by that time) had sought a path that avoided both these extremes.

The Buddha did not rest after achieving nirvana. Instead, for over four decades he helped others seek this goal as well, guiding them along the way through instruction and example. He thus embodied perfect wisdom, the result of his awakening or enlightenment; and perfect compassion, the reason for his devoting his life helping other mortals and serving as a role model of the ideal human being.

His Eightfold Path to nirvana came to be known as the Middle Way. It relied neither on penance nor poverty; nor even on the gods and deities, rituals and superstitions that were considered necessary for salvation by the Sakya clan of Hindus among whom he had first sought relief from the pervasive suffering of this world. Instead, through intense personal effort, relying solely on his own resources, he had experienced awakening. He had found that the human mind could be calmed and desire dispatched for good, leaving one free to enjoy a state of supreme happiness unsullied by pain and suffering.

The Buddha had found a new way out of man's ancient existential dilemma. In light of his path-breaking realization about the true nature of reality, the Buddha's concerns were grounded in the here and now. He had identified greed, hatred, and delusion as the primary human failings; and had realized that all three led to suffering (*dukha*). His own experience had shown that the right kind of meditation on the human condition and on the world "as it really is" was sufficient to overcome suffering. Done properly, it was able to rid the mind of ignorance, aggression, jealousy, passion, and pride, thus enabling man's natural wisdom and goodness to take hold of head and heart.

The Buddha's teachings, in his native dialect of the Pali language, were remembered and transmitted orally by his community of monks (the *sangha*) for several centuries. In the 1st century BCE they were recorded in Sri Lanka on palm leaf manuscripts, and are the basis for Theravada Buddhism (the Way of the Elders), which follows the Buddha's original teachings. Monks and nuns who could devote themselves fully and wholeheartedly to the pursuit of nirvana were able to follow these instructions as originally taught. Others—the vast majority of the people who were unable to get away from family life and found it hard to join the sangha—earned their merit (good karma) by supporting the monks with food, clothing, and shelter.

The sangha spread the Buddha's message widely, making him the founder of a thriving religion that attracted new followers from among Hindus, Jains, and animist believers. A few sects developed, with variations in belief and practice influenced by the diverse indigenous traditions of local communities, but initially these remained small and inconsequential. Over time, Buddhist texts were assembled into the Pali canon (the *Tipitaka*), which has three sections or "baskets." These texts are considered scripture by all Buddhists.

BELIEFS AND PRACTICES

THE BUDDHA TAUGHT that nirvana could be achieved by

man's efforts alone, without having to rely on God, the Supreme Reality, as his own personal experience had shown. To understand the "true nature" of things, all that was required was belief in the Buddha's teachings (the Buddha *dharma*); correctly following his Eightfold Path with disciplined mindfulness; and compassionate support from the community of Buddhist monks and nuns (the *sangha*) that he had established.

Newcomers to the religion were required to live by the simple creed, known as the Three Jewels: "I take refuge in the Buddha. I take refuge in the Dharma. I take refuge in the Sangha." The Buddha's last instruction to his disciples was to work out their own salvation with diligence.

The Buddhist goal was neither absorption nor union with *Brahman* (God, in Hinduism) but nirvana, the result of blowing out all the fires of longing and attachment that burn within every human heart. This state of nirvana was imperishable and secure, and was characterized by pure bliss and happiness. It was very different from everything else in this world—which is impermanent, constantly changing, not dependable, and the source of great grief.

The Buddha had "awakened" to the insight that desire or craving (*tanha*) for something permanent in a constantly-transient world was the source of all suffering. The complete absence of craving was a pre-requisite for complete contentment. Even the many Hindu gods were mere transitory forms that only appeared to be all-powerful. They had no lasting presence, and could not be relied upon to grant escape from the cycle of rebirth. And, in any case, the individual soul too was a transitory phenomenon, so there was really nothing—"no-thing", not even a spirit or soul of the kind accepted by his

Brahmanic contemporaries—that could continue from body to body on its unending cycle of reincarnation.

Nevertheless, the Buddha accepted that all sentient beings are caught in the cycle of rebirth, and are subject to *karma*, the moral law of cause and effect that applies to everything, including the universe itself. Positive actions count as assets, and negative ones as liabilities in the merit ledger; and both types of deeds have consequences. He and his followers sought not only to build more assets than liabilities, but to gain release from the law of karma altogether. They differed from Hinduism in how this liberation—*moksha* for Hindus, *nirvana* for Buddhists—was to be achieved; and on the nature of the soul (*atman*) that transmigrates upon rebirth into new life (since for Buddhists, even the soul was impermanent).

Initially, Buddhism had none of the features usually associated with most religions. It did not appeal to a higher authority, did not rely on rituals and tradition, did not provide explanations or speculative theories about our origins and ultimate destination, and did not rely on faith in God's grace and mystery. Instead, the Buddha asked that each individual rely only on his/her own experience and intense effort, and on no greater authority; base his search for nirvana and release from suffering on reason and empirical validation, not on ritual or superstition or tradition; not be distracted by unanswerable metaphysical questions (which he considered "not-relevant"); focus on the here and now, rather than on some presumed afterlife; and place no faith in a transcendental God whose ways would always remain mysterious and unfathomable.

Instead of the practice of yoga, asceticism, or any of the other ritualistic ways followed by the people around him, the Buddha put forth a very different point of view. The Four Noble Truths that he had realized under the *bodhi* tree (of wisdom) and preached in his first sermon at Sarnath were that suffering (*dukha*) exists; there is a reason for suffering; there is a way to end suffering; and the way to end suffering was the Eightfold Path that he, the Buddha, had found.

This Path, with eight essential aspects that were to be followed at all times, combined the "right" beliefs, moral actions, and disciplined effort. It required the right views and right thoughts (belief in the Buddha's teachings); right speech, right action, right livelihood, and right effort (thus leading to a moral life); and right mindfulness and right concentration (by exercising personal discipline). In so doing, one followed the Buddha's footsteps. Accepting his moral and spiritual teachings, living an ethical life, and treating others as you yourself would wish to be treated enabled the follower of the Buddha to make progress towards enlightenment.

The Buddha taught that knowledge and understanding of the Four Noble Truths allowed one to let go of attachments and desires. Leading a moral life required being kind and truthful, not stealing or cheating, not harming yourself or others through day-to-day activities, and maintaining a positive focus and attitude. Mindful meditation made you aware of how you affect the world, and of the consequences of your actions. Concentrating on attentively following all aspects of the Eightfold Path helped eliminate craving, which is the source of suffering. All these practices, together, led to the state of eternal peace and contentment that is necessary for attaining nirvana.

The practice of meditation and spiritual exercise was considered an essential aspect of the path to enlightenment, for it enabled the seeker to focus within the self rather than on external reality. It helped one realize how everything in the world, including the self, is impermanent and transitory; and it shifted one's attention from mere ideas and beliefs to actual personal experience. Deep meditation ultimately led to the awareness that nirvana is a state of the "non-self," and not an empty space in the external world or in the heavens beyond.

Thus, according to the Buddha, the Eightfold Path led to both infinite wisdom and unending compassion; and for this to happen, none of the Hindu (or any other) gods had a role to play. The Buddha had no need for idols and deities as symbols of the Supreme Being, nor for Brahmin priests as intermediaries, sacrifices as offerings, and Hindu rituals as modes of worship. Instead, he asked his followers to rely solely on themselves, the Buddha, the dharma, and the sangha. Meritorious deeds, and not the caste of one's parents, determined an individual's spiritual accomplishments as well as societal status. Buddhism thus was a very different religion from the Hinduism into which Siddhartha Gautama had been born.

Roots and Branches

By the first century CE—roughly six hundred years after the Buddha first taught in northern India—a new branch called Mahayana Buddhism (the Great Vehicle) had evolved. It maintained the centrality of the Buddha's teachings in the form of texts (*sutras*), but interpreted them more broadly to include aspects that shared some similarities with Hinduism. These included the deification of the Buddha, worship of his physical relics, pilgrimage to places associated with his life, and introduction of rituals and practices that resonated with Hindu society. With the passage of time, the Buddha had come to be revered by some Buddhists as a God, and by Hindus as the ninth incarnation (*avatar*) of their Lord Vishnu—even though the Buddha had insisted that he was only human in every aspect.

Theravada Buddhism had accepted the notion of an *arhat*—one who had extinguished all desire, and was thus on the cusp of Buddha-hood. Mahayana Buddhism also developed the idea of the *bodhisattva*—one who has potential to become a Buddha, is near full-enlightenment, but delays taking this step in order to compassionately help others struggling to be freed from the cycle of rebirth.

In Mahayana Buddhism, the strict monastic rules and traditions of the early Buddhist monks were modified to allow for varying degrees of commitment to the Eightfold Path. This made it easier for the lay masses to follow in the Buddha's footsteps; and helped spread Buddhism throughout India, and subsequently beyond its shores. The Mahayana scripture was written in Sanskrit, an ancient Indian language in which the *Vedas*, the earliest sacred texts of the Hindus, were also written.

Theravada and Mahayana Buddhism spread extensively within India, especially after Buddhism was embraced by Emperor Ashoka Maurya who ruled over most of India from 268 BCE to 233 BCE. It became a major religion of the sub-continent, along with Hinduism. Both branches of Buddhism retained their hold over the people of India for over fifteen hundred years, until about the 13th

century CE, when the resurgence of Hinduism and the advent of Islam displaced Buddhism from the land of its birth. By then, Theravada Buddhism had become firmly established in many neighboring countries, particularly Sri Lanka, Burma, Thailand, and Cambodia where it continues to thrive.

Mahayana Buddhism had also spread along the "silk route" that extended from India to China, covering Afghanistan, Central Asia, Mongolia, and China. The first Buddhist missionaries arrived in China in the 1st century CE. The Pure Land sects arose in China during the 5th to 7th centuries CE, and Chinese Buddhism peaked during the Tang dynasty (589 CE to 845 CE), after which there was a great persecution of Buddhism, followed by a recent revival.

From China, some sects of Buddhism spread to Korea and Japan, where they reached during the 12th century CE. Wherever it went, Buddhism adapted to the local religion, culture, and customs. The Pure Land, Nichiren, and Zen sects of Buddhism were formed in Japan around 1200 CE. The Pure Land School relied on the bodhisattva named Amida (Amitabha) to ferry followers to the Pure Land (a kind of heaven). Control of Buddhism by the Tokugawa shogunate in Japan lasted for more than 250 years, from 1603 CE to 1867 CE.

Other schools combined Buddhism with elements of Confucianism or Taoism. These included the Ti'en Tai in China (Tendai in Japan), and Ch'an (Zen) in Japan, which has recently developed a following in Western countries. In the past few centuries, Buddhism has also achieved a revival in India; and has become popular in Europe and

North America, where increasing numbers of laypersons practice various forms of yoga and meditation.

In Tibet, a third branch of Buddhism, known as Vajrayana (the Diamond Way), developed during the period 320 CE to 550 CE. This relied on sacred texts that emphasize the inter-relatedness of everything. It followed *tantric* practices that seek to harness all energies latent in human beings, including sexual energy (tantric sex), to achieve nirvana within just one lifetime. Also utilized are *mantras* (holy sounds that are chanted) and *mudras* (choreographed hand gestures). The Tibetan Dalai Lama, who has been incarnated thirteen times in the past few centuries, is the head of this branch of Buddhism. He is revered as a Bodhisattva, but is not considered a Pope because he does not define doctrine.

The practice of meditation, in its many forms, is emphasized in all branches of Buddhism. In Mahayana and Vajrayana Buddhism, which appeal especially to the masses, the chanting of mantras in the temple and at home, accompanied by the spinning of prayer wheels and the ritualistic burning of incense, helps the mind concentrate and get in sync with the sights and sounds of prayerful worship of the Buddha as a source of wisdom and as a God.

Ironically, as Buddhism evolved, it came to include many aspects of religion, traditionally conceived—which the Buddha had explicitly excluded. The religion underwent major transformation as Mahayana Buddhism emerged around the second century BCE, and continued to evolve for the next twelve hundred years. Now, among many devotional Buddhist groups, the Buddha is worshiped much like a savior God. Even some bodhisattvas (some of whom are female) are considered the "supreme authority" to whom their followers pray, and whose blessings they seek. Rituals, chanting of mantras, and prostration before statues of the deity Buddha have gained prominence, especially in Mahayana and Vajrayana Buddhism.

Also, for some Buddhists, nirvana now seems to be sought as a destination, much like heaven. The Buddha and bodhisattvas are believed to help one reach this goal through their grace and personal intercession. Yogic exercise, supplemented with meditation in its many forms, is sometimes seen as the path to blissful peace. Many of these features, added during the course of over two millennia, are new interpretations of the Buddha's original teachings, and go far beyond the strict requirements of the Eightfold Path. The Buddhism practiced in China or Japan is in many ways quite different from the Buddhism practiced today in Tibet or Sri Lanka, though each of these variations traces its roots to the insights provided by the Buddha himself.

Of course, most beliefs and practices are not universally shared by all Buddhists everywhere. There are significant differences among the various branches and sub-sects. In Theravada Buddhism for example, the individual depends on his own efforts guided by the Buddha's *dharma* (teachings and exemplary life) and supported by the *sangha* (the Buddhist monastic order). He seeks enlightenment—meaning insight into the true nature of reality—so that he may overcome the suffering that pervades life. The Buddha, as a sage, is the source of wisdom; and the goal is to become an *arhat*, a disciple who attains *nirvana* through intense personal effort and concentration. This branch of Buddhism is more suited for monks and nuns capable of and committed to dedicated effort over long periods of time, even a lifetime.

In contrast, in Mahayana Buddhism, monks and lay individuals alike seek support from others—from the bodhisattva, who having reached his goal is willing to help others, and from the Buddha as a savior (God) who could shower the seeker with his grace. Enlightenment and wisdom are still pursued, but of equal importance is the cultivation of compassion (*karuna*) which was the hallmark of the Buddha himself. The goal is to become a bodhisattva who is willing to delay or voluntarily renounce the achievement of nirvana so as to remain in this world to help others. This branch of Buddhism is more suited to laypersons who know they cannot do it alone, know they have to seek the help of others, and are willing to help them in return.

Other key differences are that while the Theravadins follow the Buddha in considering metaphysical speculation irrelevant—for "the question does not fit the case," as the Buddha used to say—the Mahayanists have developed elaborate cosmologies of multi-leveled heavens and hells. The followers of Theravada Buddhism rely primarily on meditation, as the Buddha had done; while those who follow Mahayana Buddhism rely also on supplication and petition, and call on the Buddha (as a God) and bodhisattvas for spiritual strength.

Thus, Theravada Buddhists have conserved Buddhism largely in its original form; while the Mahayana, Vajrayana, Zen, and other Buddhists have embraced new features, including less-strict disciplinary rules and new modes of practice and worship. Importantly, some Mahayana Buddhists consider later texts—known as the

Prajnaparamita or Perfection of Wisdom—as equally authoritative as the Pali canon (the *Tipitaka*) that records the original teachings of the Buddha.

Non-Theravada branches of Buddhism and their sacred texts have thus introduced beliefs and practices that interpret traditional Buddhist teachings of the Eightfold Path in new ways. On the surface, some of these beliefs seem akin to non-dualistic (*advaita*) Hinduism, especially when they appear to blur the essential distinction between this world and the next. But they are all, of course, very different from Hinduism—for they rely only on the Buddha and others inspired by him, and not on any Hindu God.

Chapter 7

Confucianism, Taoism, and Shintoism

Confucianism

CREATION AND EVOLUTION

MORE THAN TWENTY-FIVE centuries ago in China, the sage Confucius proposed a moral philosophy for harmonious living and social cohesion. In so doing, Confucius created the basis for a new cultural tradition and way of life. His ideas gradually took root over the course of several centuries, and evolved to include various aspects of local indigenous traditions as well as Buddhism. Though founded by a sage and not a prophet (messenger of God), the Confucian religion is now practiced by many of the 1.3 billion Chinese living in China and other countries.

Confucius (Kung Fu-tzu) was born around 551 BCE in the principality of Lu in modern Shantung province, and died in 479 BCE. The moral philosophy proposed by him after many decades of dedicated public service and learning was not readily accepted. After trying unsuccessfully for thirteen years to convert local feudal rulers to his way of thinking, Confucius returned home at the age of sixty-eight to devote his life to teaching a small group of devoted disciples.

Upon his death, Confucius was glorified; and within a few centuries, his teachings had been recorded in a text known as the *Analects* (the *Lun yu*). This volume, comprised of twenty small "books" (sections) totaling only a hundred pages or so in its English translation, is the only reliable record of Confucian sayings. It has served as the sacred text of Confucianism for over two millennia.

The ideas proposed by Confucius in the 5th century BCE were developed by others, notably Mencius (372-289 BCE) and Zhuang-zi (369-286 BCE). During the Han dynasty, Confucianism became the state religion; and in 130 BCE Confucian texts were the basis for training government officials. Though there had been nothing other-worldly about Confucius, some quasi-official attempts were made centuries after his death to elevate him to divine status. In 59 CE, sacrifices were offered to Confucius; and in the 7th and 8th centuries CE, temples were erected throughout the country to pay homage to him and his main disciples.

By this time, Confucianism had evolved as well, in part by incorporating various aspects of Chinese culture and social traditions, which were themselves changing.

Buddhist missionaries from India had arrived in China during the 1st century CE; and during the 5th to 7th centuries CE, there arose the Pure Land, Chan, and other religious sects in China. Buddhism flourished alongside Confucianism; and though it was severely persecuted in the years immediately following 845 CE, it dominated China from the 5th to 10th centuries CE.

However, Neo-Confucianism then gained ground on Buddhism, and re-emerged to dominate China during the 11th to 19th centuries CE. Alongside Confucianism, other indigenous traditions, as well as Buddhism, continued to be practiced too. Thus, for almost two thousand years, the Chinese have lived by a syncretic blend of shamanistic folk traditions, supplemented with Confucian ethics in public life, Taoist influences in private life, and Buddhist traditions at the time of birth and death.

BELIEFS AND PRACTICES

CONFUCIUS'S CENTRAL CONCERN was man and his relationships with fellow humans. God does not figure much in Confucian thought, for Confucius asks that in meeting his moral responsibility, man think for and rely only upon himself. The goal of self-cultivation is to become more-completely human, and improve society as well, by expanding one's capacity for sympathy and empathy (*hsin*) indefinitely. Both (inner) personal growth and (outer) concern for others' welfare are essential for fully-actualizing human potential.

The ideal person (*chun tzu*, gentleman or mature person) has impeccable moral character and is full of virtue (*te*) and benevolence (*jen*). Virtue is partly a gift from "Heaven" (*t'ien*)—the power of moral example or inherent righteousness of our ancestral spirits, an idea that pre-dated Confucianism by over 500 years; or is fated by Destiny (*ming*)—that which brings about what must come to pass ("what will be, will be").

In contrast, benevolence is a trait acquired through man's own efforts and conscious attention. A benevolent man follows the so-called "golden rule" of moral behavior. "Do not impose on others what you yourself do not desire." (the *Analects*, XII.2 and XV.24); also translated as "What you do not wish done to yourself, do not do to others." A benevolent man's success in following this rule depends solely on his own self.

However, according to Confucius, yogic saintliness in remote isolation is also not right, for the "self" withers without social relationships. Man has to learn to thrive in relationships with his fellow men. Benevolence or "human-heartedness" shows up in love and respect towards oneself and others, and is accompanied by magnanimity, good faith, and charity.

Such a person acts in accordance with proper rites and rituals (*li*, body of rules), and does what is right—i.e., in line with the Way of the universe (the Truth), and how it is meant to be done. Different ways are prescribed for individuals occupying different roles, such as king, master, nobleman, gentleman, or "small man" (*hsio jen*, common person). The five key relationships are between parent and child, husband and wife, elder and younger sibling, elder and junior friend, and ruler and subject. Natural love and reciprocal family and social obligations are the basis of family-, clan- and society-wide morality.

The hard-to-achieve but only worthwhile goal is to become and act like a morally-good person (a "gentleman"; presumably, a gentlewoman too). This goal is to be pursued for its own sake, devoid of any self-interest. No worldly rewards are to be expected, nor is survival after this life of any consequence, for Confucius is agnostic about death and what, if anything, comes after it. Attaining "heaven" in an afterlife, as a reward for good behavior, is not the reason for living a moral life.

Besides benevolence, other virtues prized in a "gentleman" are wisdom, intelligence, and courage. A wise person knows right from wrong, is a good judge of character, acquires knowledge through learning, and is honest, truthful, reliable, trustworthy in word and deed, and respectful towards others. He takes seriously his responsibility for promoting the common man's welfare, which is also the government's ultimate purpose. Courage is a virtue only when engaged in moral actions, i.e., when doing the right thing, not otherwise. Morals can be transmitted from teacher to pupil, but a ruler must set a moral example, for deeds matter more than words. As times change, so must the rights and wrongs, and the rules and rites.

It was this new ethical philosophy of social harmony that Confucius championed—and the Chinese have followed for over two millennia. Some Confucian ideas have been modified through interaction with other cultural traditions or emerging beliefs—such as Taoism in China and Shintoism in Japan—but no distinct and widely-followed Confucian sects have emerged. The original teachings of Confucius, the great sage, have thus endured, not only as a social philosophy but as a recognizable religion with growing numbers and influence throughout the world.

Taoism

Lao Tzu, the founder of Taoism (pronounced Daoism), was born around 604 BCE in China, but little is known about his life. He did not teach or preach, organize or promote; and all his ideas are contained in a slim volume of only five thousand Chinese characters compiled in the 3rd century CE. This short book (of less than fifty pages) is titled the *Tao Te Ching* (pronounced Dow Deh Jing); in English, "The Way and its Power" or "The Book of the Way", since *Tao* means the path or way.

The Tao Te Ching, the main scripture of Taoism, is essentially a deeply-philosophical manual on the art of living morally and for caring for the welfare of one's fellow human beings. It teaches simplicity, patience, and compassion; as well as softness, suppleness, adaptability, freedom, and endurance.

The *Tao* is to be understood as the way of the mysterious, ineffable, transcendent, and immanent ultimate reality from which all life springs and to which it returns; and also as the way of human life when it is in harmony with the Tao of the universe. A special meditative prayer completes the ritual cycle of rebirth, and brings about union with the transcendent Tao.

The *Te* (power) is multifaceted; and not one but three

types of Taoism, all dissimilar, have evolved in China over the centuries. The three species are philosophical, religious, and "augmented" Taoism. Philosophic Taosim is more like a reflective self-help program; and Augmented Taoism seeks to maximize vital energy (*ch'i*) by working with the mind, matter, and movement (*t'ai ch'i*) through such means as meditation and yoga. Both these types of Taoism are less suitable for the masses than Religious Taoism, which is more popular, and developed its own church, priesthood and rituals in the second century CE. Despite these differences, all three types of Taoism are based on the *Tao Te Ching*, the religion's sacred text.

Taoism is also concerned with rituals and attitudes towards nature—and there are many treatises, tracts, and manuals that provide relevant guidance on a variety of topics. They include texts for performing rituals for exorcism and healing, for practicing herbal medicine and alchemy, and for acting in accordance with local mythology and indigenous religious practices.

In many ways, Taoism is the opposite of Confucianism. They both seek balance and harmony, but they reach this goal in very different ways. Taoism has a more holistic approach, balancing life's opposites—the *yin* and *yang*— and resolving their inherent tension through the power of the eternal wholeness of Tao. It also emphasizes the relativity of good and evil, and the complementarity of opposites, such as light and dark, positive and negative, male and female.

In China, this complementarity can be seen in the interplay of Taoism and Confucianism as well. While Taoism favors spontaneity and naturalness, Confucianism stresses social responsibility; and while Confucianism focuses on the human, Taoism goes far beyond. Both approaches are valuable, and are highly respected and popular in China. Hence, the remarkable influence of Taoism has been felt in the lives of ordinary Chinese folk for over two millennia, despite the dominance of Confucianism and Buddhism at various periods of Chinese history.

Shintoism

SHINTOISM IS THE indigenous religion of Japan. It has traditionally been practiced in three forms: folk Shinto, shrine Shinto, and sect Shinto. In earlier times, festivals were important, especially for praying for or celebrating a good harvest; and divination and purification rites were important features too.

Shintoism seeks to unite mankind with divine beings known as *kami*—who desire that people enjoy communal harmony and abundance, as well as increased productivity, creativity, and prosperity. The *kami* are of various types, such as the kami of nature, ideas, places, and people (the living kami). Clan kami are associated with rites for ancestors; and charismatic kami with local shrines that are objects of faith.

Priests play a key role in Shintoism. Traditionally, the Japanese Emperor was especially important, for he was the chief priest of the Shinto world. In ancient times, the reigning emperor or empress was believed to have mystical powers to receive influences from the sun goddess, increase the food supply, and thereby improve the welfare of the common people.

In Japan, Shintoism has been intertwined with Confucianism and Buddhism for about fifteen hundred years. Both these religions were introduced into Japan from China in around the 5th century CE; and over the next one thousand years, new Buddhist sects that were influenced by Shintiosm developed. Of these, the Nara, Tendai, and Shingon sects of Buddhism were introduced from China between the 7th and 9th centuries CE; and the Pure Land, True Pure Land, Nichiren, and Zen sects were founded in Japan around 1200 CE.

The Tendai sect in Japan gives special importance to the *Lotus Sutra*, according to which all forms of existence, animate and inanimate, have an innate Buddha nature. Humans can become a living Buddha in one lifetime, without having to go through the cycle of rebirth. The Kukai sect, based on Tantric Buddhism in China, believes that meditation, ritual postures, and mystical chants are able to connect man to the living substance of the cosmos. Some of these beliefs have been subtly influenced by Shintoism.

Some other Buddhist sects, such as the Pure Land, simply rely on the power and compassion of Amida (Amitabha) Buddha for deliverance of all people. The True Pure Land sect believes that simple faith in Amitabha is enough for gaining entry into the Pure Land; and austerities of any kind, celibacy, and the monastic life are not required. These beliefs draw upon Shinto traditional beliefs to some extent. Thus, Shintoism and other religions have influenced one another in Japan for many centuries.

Though Buddhism was centrally controlled by the Tokugawa shogunate during 1603-1867 CE, and various other smaller "New religions" emerged after 1814 CE, Shintoism dominated as a State religion in Japan from the mid-nineteenth century until 1945 CE, the end of World War II. Now Shintoism is no longer a state religion, but it continues to thrive as a set of firmly-held religious beliefs and practices, mainly in Japan.

Chapter 8

Christianity

CREATION AND EVOLUTION

CHRISTIANITY TRACES ITS roots to the prophet Jesus, the Messiah (*Christos* in Greek), who was born in about 4 BCE, lived for about thirty-three years, and preached to his Jewish followers for the last three years of his life. Three days after his death, Jesus was bodily resurrected by the Lord (God), his Father, and ascended to Heaven to reign by His side. Jesus did not leave behind a written text; but the main events and messages of his life were recorded by his followers, conveying the good news (gospel) of His birth, life, Crucifixion, Resurrection, and Ascension. These stories—and God's messages revealed to the Lord Jesus Christ—are recorded in the *New Testament* of the Christian *Holy Bible*.

According to the Bible, Jesus was born in Bethlehem to a Jewish virgin named Mary, whose husband was the carpenter Joseph of Nazareth. Mary had immaculately conceived Jesus with the divine intercession of the Holy Spirit (God); and during his life on earth, Jesus healed the sick, performed miracles, taught new ways of fulfilling the Laws of Moses, and preached a new message from the loving God to mankind. Jesus was crucified by the Romans as punishment for charges brought against him by the high priests of the Jewish Temple in Jerusalem who did not accept his teachings. He died on the cross in Jerusalem, in Palestine.

The prophet Jesus preached only to his own Jewish community. After his death, his disciple Paul extended his teachings and religious message to non-Jews (gentiles) as well; but during the first century CE, Christianity was simply one sect of non-rabbinic Judaism. Gradually, over time, Christians began to believe that Jesus had died for the sins of all mankind; and that with his death and resurrection, the sins of all who believed in him—that is, those who became Christians—would be forgiven, and their eternal life after death would be assured if they lived as faithful Christians.

The Christian Bible records that, as taught by Jesus, some Mosaic laws and Jewish traditions, such as keeping the Sabbath, did not have to be strictly followed. In addition, Paul did not insist that male followers of Jesus be circumcised, as was required by the Jewish faith within which Jesus had preached. Since the Judaic tradition emphasized faithful observance of all the commandments of the Hebrew Bible, the ties with Judaism were considerably loosened. Paul's message appealed to some Jews and gentiles alike, and helped grow the Christian Church.

During the centuries following Jesus' death, several groups came into being whose beliefs and practices were part-Jewish and part-Christian. However, perseverance by the inspired leaders of the nascent Church enabled the main message of Christianity to get through to the laity. The evolution of both Judaic and Christian beliefs continued concurrently throughout the early centuries of the 1st millennium CE—and Rabbinic Judaism and Christianity took shape side by side. These developments made the distinctive features of both these religions much clearer, and enabled Christianity to establish a separate identity for itself.

The native tongue spoken by Jesus and his immediate disciples was Aramaic. However, before the birth of Jesus, the Hebrew Bible had been translated into Greek; and it was the Greek version that was known to Jesus and his Jewish followers. The four gospels of the Christian Bible were originally written in Greek, in about 65 CE to 95 CE. The exact authorship of the gospels is not known; but the accounts of the life of Jesus included in the Bible are ascribed to Matthew, Mark, Luke, and John, who were not direct disciples of Jesus. Other books of the New Testament, also in Greek, were written and edited by other followers during the three centuries that followed.

The sixty-six books of the Christian Bible include the *Old Testament*, which consists of books of the Hebrew Bible, beginning with the five books of Moses. It took several centuries of compilation, editing, debate, and fine-tuning before the books of the *New Testament* could be finalized into a widely-accepted version. The Christian Bible finally accepted as canon by Church authorities was translated in around 384 CE from Greek into Latin (this version is known as the *Vulgate*), and into English a thousand years later, in 1388 CE. The King James' version of the Bible was first produced in English in 1611 CE.

The task of faithfully translating the Hebrew and Greek versions of the Christian Bible and producing the "authorized" English version was undertaken by forty-seven scholars appointed by King James of England. It remains the standard text for everyday use in churches and homes in the English-speaking world, though other versions of the Christian Bible, in English as well as in other languages, are also available. In the English version, the Old Testament (the Hebrew Bible of the Jewish faith) is three times the length of the New Testament of Jesus Christ. The Old Testament has thirty-nine books covering more than 1180 pages, while the New Testament has twenty-seven books covering about 400 pages. Both Testaments are fundamental to the Christian faith, are viewed as integral parts of one *Holy Bible*, and together constitute Christian scripture.

BELIEFS AND PRACTICES

ACCORDING TO CHRISTIANS, the Old Testament prophecy of the coming of the Messiah is fulfilled in the story of Jesus, as revealed in the New Testament. According to some believers, the Christian Bible reveals the Truth, the literal Word of God. The last book of the New Testament, titled "Revelation," also includes a prophecy about the second coming of Jesus as Messiah and Savior of mankind at the end of time.

Christians believe that with the coming of Jesus, a new covenant was reached with God, as is recorded in the New Testament. In this Testament, it is revealed that Jesus had come to this world to bring the love, grace, and mercy of God to all mankind, and to provide salvation and redemption to those who believe in him as the Christ, the Anointed One. The Judaic beliefs in the soul, afterlife, heaven, hell, Last Day of Judgment, faith in the Lord, and the responsibility and benefits of living a moral life were maintained; and in dealings with fellow Christians, love, charity, humility, neighborliness, social justice, and tolerance of differences were emphasized.

Early Christians also adapted their Jewish traditions to the new message of salvation through Jesus Christ. The Jewish celebration of Passover commemorating the Jews' Exodus from Egypt became the Christian Holy Eucharist celebrating the sacrifice of Jesus on the cross; and His body and blood signified a new Exodus from sin and death to life with God. The rite of circumcision was replaced by baptism, signifying entry into a new covenant with the Lord, replacing the old life outside the Church with a new life in Christ.

The evolution of Christian doctrine continued for several centuries after the life, death, and resurrection of Jesus. The books of the New Testament had revealed Jesus' closeness to God. Jesus had spoken of God as Father, distinct from himself, the son of God. But he had also said: "Anyone who has seen me has seen the Father" (the *New Testament*, John 14:9); and "the Father and I are one" (John 10:30). Some of his disciples had said: "Today in the town of David a Savior has been born to you; he is Christ the Lord." (Luke 2:11); and "God was in Christ reconciling the world to Himself." (2 Corinthians 5:19)

Understandably, these Christian beliefs were initially

controversial. According to the gospels, Jesus had been born to a Jewish mother named Mary, had been raised in a Jewish family, had taught from the Hebrew Bible, and had died as a Jewish believer and preacher. Some sayings attributed to him by his disciples contradicted established Jewish belief in the one God (*Yahweh*) who did not incarnate in human form, and who did not have a Father or son.

Jesus had been a Jewish preacher; and the new Christian beliefs were obviously inconsistent with traditional Jewish beliefs. Attempts to reconcile them led to a variety of views. To resolve issues stemming from different interpretations of fundamental doctrine that had emerged over time, Christian bishops were asked by the Church to assemble on a number of occasions to discuss matters related to the divinity of Jesus the man, who had been born as son of God, and was himself God.

The Christian Councils held in Nicaea in 325 CE, in Constantinople in 381 CE, and in Chalcedon in 451 CE pronounced that Jesus was fully-divine, and had taken fully-human form to atone for man's sins. Jesus, the Son of God, Lord of all Creation, born to the Virgin Mary, was of the same substance as His Father. His crucifixion, in which God had sacrificed His only begotten Son, demonstrated God's love for mankind. The Almighty God, the Lord Jesus Christ, and the Holy Spirit together formed the Holy Trinity.

This belief, known as the Nicene Creed, was slightly modified by later Councils, but it succinctly expressed core orthodox Christian beliefs of that time. By the 6th century CE it had been accepted as the foundational core doctrine of the Christian Church. This doctrine was based on complete faith in Jesus Christ and his teachings, as recorded by his disciples in the Christian Bible. The scripture thus became central to the life of the Church; and has since then become enormously important for all followers of Jesus Christ.

According to this Bible, Christianity offers hope of salvation in this life and the next. The text of Revelation—the only book of prophecy in the New Testament—reveals that towards the end of time, Jesus will return to earth in glory to establish God's peaceful and joyous kingdom that will last a thousand years. On the Last Day of Judgment, every human, living or dead, will be judged individually by Jesus, and everyone will reap what he/she has sown.

During the Apocalypse, after much violence, disease and pestilence, the righteous Lord Jesus Christ will ultimately triumph over the utterly-evil and satanic Antichrist. Christians will be forgiven their sins, and will ascend to Heaven with their Savior and Redeemer Jesus Christ, to live forever in peace and happiness with Almighty God. Non-Christians will descend into the hot fires of Hell, to suffer eternal torment and damnation with the devil Satan.

Roots and Branches

By the 4ᵀᴴ century CE, Christians had spread far beyond Palestine; and in 313 CE the Roman rulers announced a state policy of religious tolerance towards Christianity. With a reduction in official persecution of Christians, and especially after Emperor Constantine's baptism on his deathbed in 337 CE, Christianity became firmly established as the religion of the Roman Empire, and as a major faith in the Mediterranean region.

After the Roman Empire formally embraced Christianity, the religion spread to other parts of Europe and Central Asia. The Holy Bible served to bind all Christians into one Church. Later, however, new sects began to emerge; and in 1054 CE the eastern and western parts of the Roman Church split into two, and this led to the formation of two main sects of Christianity—the Eastern Orthodox Church and the Catholic Church.

A further split took place in the 16th century during the Reformation, when Protestants broke away from the western Catholic Church to form their own Church. Protestants further divided into Mennonites and Lutherans in 1517 CE and Anglicans in 1536 CE. Then the Lutheran Church split in 1566 CE to form the Calvinists; and the Anglican Church split during subsequent centuries to form the Methodists, Episcopalians, Baptists, Presbyterians, Congregationalists, and Quakers.

In these sects of Christianity, the main rites and sacraments are carried out somewhat differently, or have different significance or symbolism. The sects have important similarities too. All Christians have faith in the Lord Jesus Christ as their Savior, and consider the Christian Bible as their sacred and authoritative scripture. And for all Christians, baptism is the means of becoming a Christian and accepting God's forgiveness; at Mass (or the Eucharist) they share bread (representing Jesus' body) and wine (representing His blood) in remembrance of His death and resurrection; at Confession, a priest has the authority to hear a confession of sins or wrongdoing, and to grant forgiveness in the name of God; and marriage vows are made before Jesus Christ, the Lord.

The mutual tolerance, as well as occasional violent conflict, among the various Christian sects are noteworthy. The split within the "eastern" Church, as well as the Reformation of the Catholic Church, were due to both ideological and theological reasons that have continued to affect the course of Christian history over centuries. Some sects differ on their understanding of the person of Christ and his nature as both human and divine, as well as on various aspects of Christian beliefs and practice that obviously matter a great deal to sectarian followers.

The Orthodox Church, for example, considers the original Nicene Creed and traditional Christian practices central to its faith. In contrast, the Eastern Orthodox Church, which too claims direct descent from Jesus and the apostles, gives primacy to liturgy over doctrine, and considers many beliefs and practices of the Catholic and Protestant churches inappropriate innovations. In the Eastern Orthodox Church, the incarnation of God in Christ is accepted, but the dogmas of the immaculate conception of Mary, her bodily "Assumption" to heaven, and the infallibility of the Catholic Pope as "vicar of Christ on earth" are not. Purgatory is denied, but prayers are offered to the dead, who can and do pray for the living. Liturgy is conducted in Greek—the language of the original New Testament of Jesus Christ—and is accompanied by elaborate forms of ritualistic worship.

Similarly, differences in beliefs and practice are found among the "western" Christian Churches. The Catholic Church has always looked to Rome for guidance; and it conducted liturgy in Latin until recent times. Its doctrine was largely established during the time between the original apostles and the 8th century CE; and it accepts the creeds proclaimed by various Councils of bishops. In contrast, with the Reformation in the 16th century—led by a German monk named Martin Luther, who protested against the doctrine of the Catholic Church and the practices of its priests—the allegiance of Protestants shifted from the bishop/Pope in Rome to other archbishops, and worship came to be conducted in English or other native languages.

Some of these sectarian differences were not resolved peacefully. In 1204 CE, for instance, relations between the Orthodox and Catholic Churches were nearly destroyed by the sack of Constantinople by Catholic crusaders. Several centuries later, Protestants protested against the power of the Pope in Rome and the numerous rituals the priests had introduced; and they wished to go back to the basic doctrines of the faith as canonized in scripture alone. These protests led to violent persecutions of Protestants by Catholics; followed by violent persecutions of Catholics by Protestants. Later, differences among the Protestant sects too became significant, and led to sectarian conflict in Europe that lasted several centuries, during and after the Reformation.

Most of these past conflicts have now been settled, though disagreements continue to erupt into sporadic violence from time to time. Sectarian differences are also being resolved by forming newer sects. There are now more than twenty major Christian Churches in America alone. These include, in chronological order, the Orthodox, Oriental Orthodox, Catholic, Episcopal, Anglican, Lutheran, Reformed, Congregationalist, Presbyterian,

Mennonite, Anabaptist, Friends (Quakers), Brethren, Pietist, Baptist, Methodist, Holiness, Restorationist, Adventist, Sabbatarian (Hebraic), Pentecostal, Native American, Fundamentalist, Bible, and the Community Churches. Within these, there are about two hundred Christian denominations in America; and countless others in other parts of the globe.

These Churches reflect both the religious unity of Christianity—centered on Jesus Christ and the Christian Bible—and the diversity or pluralism of Christian belief and practice. They reflect also the global spread of Christianity through mass conversion, colonization, and conquest of numerous indigenous communities through the centuries. Christians now number over two billion, making Christianity the most-widely practiced religion in the world today.

Chapter 9

Islam

CREATION AND EVOLUTION

THE PROPHET MUHAMMAD, the founder of Islam, was born in 570 CE in Mecca and died in 632 CE in Medina. In 610 CE, in a cave on Mount Hira, the angel Gabriel asked him to "Proclaim! (or Read!) In the name of thy Lord and Cherisher, Who created."(The Holy *Qur'an*, surah 96:1). Thus began a series of new revelations from *Allah* (in Arabic, *al Ilah* means *the God*).

Over a period of twenty-three years, Prophet Muhammad faithfully recited these revelations to his followers without adding anything of his own. He also showed his followers through personal example what it meant to be a Muslim, i.e., one who willingly surrenders or accepts submission (*islam*) to the Will of Allah. Islam is thus a religion of beliefs and practices that accept or conform to the (Islamic) laws of Allah; and it is also a universal religion for all who accept the Will of God, and hence are Muslims.

The main events of Prophet Muhammad's life are well known. He was born into the polytheist-animist Quraysh tribe in Arabia, was orphaned early, and was raised by his paternal uncle Abu Talib. He married several times; and his first wife, the wealthy widow Khadijah, bore him three sons who died in infancy and four daughters who continued his direct lineage. Muhammad led camel caravans to major trading points in Syria and elsewhere; and during these journeys and in Mecca, he met followers of various religions, including animist pagans, Zoroastrians, Jews, and Christians. Upon being chosen by God as His Messenger, Muhammad devoted himself to establishing the new religion of Islam and expanding the territory it covered.

Muhammad lived initially in Mecca (Makkah), a major trading center, which also housed the *Ka'bah,* the cube-shaped sanctuary built by prophet Abraham and his son Ishmael, at which 367 tribal pagan deities and idols were once worshiped. The pantheon of pre-Islamic Arabic deities was headed by the god known to pagan worshipers as Allah, and included three female goddesses who were Allah's daughters. The Ka'bah was a key pilgrimage destination for many tribes that believed in various indigenous polytheistic traditions.

After God's revelations began to descend upon him, Muhammad sought to convert members of his and other tribes to the worship of only Allah (the God). He faced strong resistance from established tribal and religious elders who believed in polytheism and did not wish to convert to the strict monotheism preached by Muhammad.

He was first recognized as a genuine prophet by his wife Khadijah, his close companion Abu Bakr, and a small but devoted group of followers. Within three years—based on continuing revelations from Allah, his own strong faith, and a message of equality and justice for all under One God—he brought together a small group of followers that accepted Islam, i.e., submission only to Allah. Following this, the monotheistic religion of Islam began to take root.

In 622 CE, Muhammad and about one hundred Muslim families moved from Mecca to the oasis settlement of Yathrib (Madinah, or Medina), where he was well received, not only by the pagan tribes but also by some powerful Jewish groups that lived there. It was from here that Prophet Muhammad spread the message of the Oneness of God, and the teachings of the Holy *Qur'an*, the Muslim sacred scripture.

Besides being the founder of a new religion, Muhammad was also an exceptional reformer, administrator, diplomat, military commander, and leader of a new community. By the time of his death, most residents of Mecca, Medina, and the surrounding areas had become Muslims; the Ka'bah had been rid of pagan idols, and had become the center of Islamic worship of the One God, Allah; and Mecca and Medina had become Islam's holiest places for prayer and pilgrimage.

Muhammad's journey from Mecca to Medina in 622 CE is known as the *Hijrah*, and marks the beginning of the Muslim calendar (1 AH, "After Hijrah"). By the end of the 7th century CE, the religion of Islam was well established, and communities of Muslims had formed throughout the Arabian Peninsula (now Saudi Arabia), and in some adjoining lands. Within a century of the establishment of the religion, Islam had spread widely in the Mediterranean region, North Africa, and the Middle East, and had even crossed the Indus river into India.

Beliefs and Practices

In Islam, only *Allah*, the One God, is worshiped; and the creedal statement is straightforward: "There is no God but Allah and Muhammad is His Prophet." ("*la ilaha illa 'l-Lah [Allah] wa Muhammadan rasulu 'l-Lah*"). Anyone who accepts this creed with faith and understanding is a Muslim.

The earlier prophets of Judaism and Christianity, including Musa (Moses), Ibrahim (Abraham), and 'Isa (Jesus) are honored as well; but it is believed that the messages revealed to them were incomplete or had been misunderstood or misinterpreted by their followers, so God sent another prophet to remind the people of the original correct message. "It is He Who sent down to thee (step by step), in truth, the Book, confirming what went before it." (Qur'an, 3:3-4); and "None of Our revelations do We abrogate or cause to be forgotten, but We substitute something better or similar." (Qur'an, 2:106).

Muhammad was not divine, but he is the last and final prophet: "Muhammad (is) the Apostle of God, and the Seal of the Prophets." (Qur'an, 33:40). The revelations conveyed to him were full, complete, uncorrupted, and final. "This is a Glorious Qur'an, (inscribed) in a Tablet Preserved!" (Qur'an, 85:21-22)

About twenty years after the demise of the Prophet,

his followers recorded these revelations in the form of a Holy book, the *Qur'an* (meaning "The Recitation" in Arabic), which contains the Word of God as originally and directly communicated in Arabic to Prophet Muhammad. The Qur'an has 114 *surahs* (chapters, containing verses), of varying length. The shorter ones, the eighty-five surahs revealed in Mecca, are placed toward the middle and end of the Qur'an, though they were the earliest revelations.

The contents of this scripture have been with Allah in heaven since eternity, before the world was created: "With Him is the Mother of the Book." (Qur'an, 13:39). They are the "uncreated" message from the One God, the Creator. The Qur'an, along with other sayings and actions of the Prophet, known as the *Hadith*—which show how the teachings of the Qur'an are to be interpreted—is the foundation of the new religion.

Muslims believe that the one and only God, *Allah*, is the Most Merciful (*al-Rahman*) and Most Compassionate (or Most Gracious, *al-Raheem*) (Qur'an, 1:1). He is the all-powerful and all-knowing Creator, most beneficent and just. The Qur'an says: "God! There is no god but He, the Living, the Self-Subsisting, Eternal." (Qur'an, 2:255 and 3:2). And also: "He is God, the One and Only; God, the Eternal, Absolute; He begetteth not, nor is He begotten; And there is none like unto Him." (Qur'an, 112:1-4).

In the Qur'an, *Allah* is spoken of with ninety-nine Names, one for each of His divine attributes. Previously, the god known as Allah (*al-Ilah*, "the deity" to the Bedouins) had been worshiped by the Babylonians as *Il* (god); by the Canaanites, and later Israelites, as *El*; and by the South Arabians as *Ilah*.

Muslims are expected to live life the way God intended, profess belief in Allah, and realize God's Will by spreading the message and law of Islam. They are expected to follow the Prophet's teachings and actions in thought, word, and deed. Allah is supreme and transcendent, but he is not remote, for He is "nearer to him [man] than (his) jugular vein." (Qur'an, 50:16). Islam expects all Muslims to follow a way of life that submits to Allah in accordance with the teachings of the Qur'an, as revealed to the Prophet Muhammad—for it is the Qur'an through which "The Word of thy Lord doth find its fulfillment in truth and in justice." (Qur'an, 6:115).

The Qur'an provides new revelations about many of the stories in the Jewish and Christian Bibles relating to the prophets Noah, Abraham, Moses, Jesus, and many others. It mentions twenty five prophets from the Hebrew Bible and the New Testament; and accepts them as God's messengers who conveyed messages suitable for their times: "For each period is a Book (revealed)." (Qur'an, 13:38). Abraham, who had submitted to the will of God, is considered the first Muslim, since he too had worshipped the one true God. (Qur'an, 3:67).

The Qur'an honors Jesus, son of the virgin Mary, as a prophet; but it does not accept Jesus as God or son of God, since Allah is One and has no equal: "No son did God beget, nor is there any god along with Him." (Qur'an, 23:91). It forbids worship of idols or deities of any kind; so images of Allah or the Prophet Muhammad are strictly prohibited. The one unforgivable sin in Islam is polytheism and idolatry (*shirk*), i.e., associating anybody or anything with God, who alone is true, unique, transcendent, and ineffable.

While accepting the prophets of Judaism and Christianity, the Qur'an makes a distinction between these religions and Islam. According to the Qur'an: "They say: "Become Jews or Christians if ye would be guided (to salvation). Say thou: Nay! (I would rather) the Religion of Abraham the True, and he joined not gods with God." (Qur'an, 2:135)…."So if they believe as ye believe, they are indeed on the right path; but if they turn back, it is they who are in schism; but God will suffice thee as against them, and He is the All-hearing, the All-knowing." (Qur'an, 2:137).

Muslims believe the Qur'an is the infallible, complete, and final revelation from God. As the original Word of God, only the Qur'an in the original Arabic is considered authentic, and its translations into other languages are considered mere interpretations. The Holy Qur'an, along with the extensive Hadith—the utterances of Muhammad whose authenticity and reliable transmission have been vouched for by the Prophet's early followers—provide guidance on spiritual as well as secular aspects of life. Together, they also form the basis of Islamic law (*Fiqh*, or *Shari'ah* law) that shows the divinely-mandated "straight path" of Islam that Muslims are required to follow.

There are several major schools of Shari'ah, i.e., codes of conduct and laws compiled by religious experts and scholars; and most Muslim live according to one of them. The main schools of law are the Hanafi, Hanbali, Maliki, Shafi (for Sunni Muslims), and Jafari, Akbari, and Usuli (for the Shi'ah), each of which dominates in different parts of the Islamic world. In addition, Muslims are guided by the example set by Prophet Muhammad in his life in Mecca and Medina, as traditionally accepted as the record of his "observed conduct" (*sunnah*). In Islam, all acts of daily life are categorized in ethical terms as obligatory, recommended, permitted, reprehensible but not forbidden, or forbidden. Breaking a provision of Islamic law is considered both a crime against society and a sin against God for which the guilty would suffer in this life and the next.

The five main beliefs of Islam are belief in one God, *Allah*; in the sacred scripture, the uncreated holy *Qur'an*; in the revered Angels; in the Prophet Muhammad and other prophets sent before him; and in the Last Day of Judgment for all mankind. On this Day, all the dead will be raised and judged by Allah. Those souls whose good outweighs the bad will gain entry into Paradise, and the others will suffer eternally in the fires of Hell. However, death is not to be feared, for it is pre-determined by Allah; and excessive mourning is discouraged since it seems to mistrust God's love and mercy. Because it would be resurrected at the end of time, the dead body is buried and not cremated.

Muslims believe also that God is everywhere; and everything happens in this world in accordance with His Will. Hence, in Islam, no distinction is made between the sacred and the secular. God is to be remembered at all times; and the Qur'an and Hadith have to be followed in all daily activities. Compassion, humility, brotherhood, equality, and peace and goodwill toward everyone are expected from all Muslims. Congregational prayers at a mosque are required only at mid-day on Fridays. On other days, one can pray anywhere, for the whole world is Allah's creation. During the *hajj*, all pilgrims—men and women—wear a simple white garment as a mark of equality with others and humility before God.

In addition, the "five pillars" of Islam are expected to be followed. These obligatory practices are declaration of faith (*shahadah*, confessing to the creed of Islam); prayer (*salat* in Arabic, *namaz* in Persian), daily at the five specified times, and at mid-day on Friday in a mosque, facing Mecca; fasting (*sawm*), daily during Ramadan, the ninth month of the Islamic lunar calendar; alms-giving or welfare-tax (*zakat*), distributed to the needy; and pilgrimage to Mecca (*hajj*), at least once in a lifetime if economic and physical circumstances permit.

Jihad is sometimes considered the sixth pillar of Islam. By jihad is meant the struggle to realize God's Will, to lead a virtuous life, and to defend and further the understanding of Islam, including through holy war, if necessary. A key moral obligation is gratitude and obedience toward Allah. Islam believes that all of humanity is one, and should therefore become a single community (*ummah*).

The earliest Muslim communities introduced social norms that were less restrictive for women than the norms then-prevalent in male-dominated patriarchal tribal society. For example, Muslim women could not be forced to marry without their explicit consent to the marriage contract. They were given inheritance rights, though less than those of Muslim men; and their legal testimony was accepted, though the testimony of two women was equal to that of one man. Women could pray at a mosque in a separate enclosed area.

Following the example set by Prophet Muhammad, Islam discouraged celibacy, and encouraged marriage as a sacred covenant. Men, but not women, could marry non-Muslims; and could divorce their wives unilaterally, though this was discouraged. Men could marry up to four wives if they could treat them fairly and equally; and in keeping with tribal traditions, women were expected to dress and behave modestly at all times.

Muslims were (and still are) expected to show kindness, respect, justice, fraternity, and equality toward fellow believers. In addition, honesty, loyalty, courage, and humility are highly-regarded personal values; and chastity, modesty, and restraint are considered obligatory for women. The Qur'an condemns practices such as female infanticide, fornication, adultery, theft, murder, usury, and exploitation of the poor. It requires that boys be circumcised (as in Judaism).

ROOTS AND BRANCHES

UPON THE PROPHET'S passing in 10 AH/632 CE, most of his followers elected the respected Abu Bakr as his successor. Abu Bakr, along with Khadijah, had been one of the earliest believers in Muhammad and was later his father-in-law. He was considered the best qualified to become the first caliph (*khalifah*) to lead the new religion in its temporal aspects, while spiritual leadership remained with the Prophet and the Qur'an. Others thought that Ali ibn Abi Talib—who was Muhammad's first cousin, close associate, and son-in-law (husband of his daughter Fatimah)—ought to be his immediate successor; and this led to conflict within the Muslim community.

The first four Caliphs were all companions of the Prophet. They provided guidance on the norms to be followed, and the actions to be emulated (*sunnah*) by the Muslim community. This guidance serves as the basis for what is known as the Sunni branch of Islam. Muhammad's son-in-law Ali became the fourth Caliph; and his followers—who believed that subsequent successors (Imams) should be Muhammad's direct descendents through Ali's son Husayn—came to be known as Shi'at 'Ali (partisans of 'Ali) or Shi'ah Muslims. Thus, the newly-established religious community split into Sunni and Shi'ah Muslims, the two main branches of Islam for the past fourteen hundred years.

The Sunnis emphasize faithful adherence to the doctrine and traditions of the Medina period, as preached and lived by the Prophet himself and continued under the first four Orthodox Caliphs. Their source of primary religious authority is the *Qur'an* and the path (sunnah) and sayings (hadith) of the Prophet. The Shi'ah too follow the Qur'an and Hadith; but they also consider the person appointed as *Imam* as the divinely-inspired infallible religious leader of the community. The Imam's legitimacy derives from the unbroken spiritual link between Allah and His chosen Messenger, Prophet Muhammad, continued through 'Ali (the Prophet's son-in-law, and the first Imam), 'Ali's son Husayn (one of the Prophet's two grandsons), and his direct descendants, nine of whom became Imams.

In the eighth century CE, an important sub-group emerged within both the Sunni and Shi'ah branches of Islam. Known as the Sufis, these followers of meditative devotion of God sought a direct experience of Allah, emphasizing the interior path of spiritual discipline instead of the exterior path of law and obedience to the

Will of Allah (*shari'ah*). Sufis practice asceticism and mysticism, seeking oneness with Allah, emphasizing the immanence rather than the transcendence of God.

Their aim is to spiritually unite during this life itself with that bit of the Creator that dwells in every human being. This approach differs from the Sunni's Shari'ah, according to which knowledge of and adherence to the teachings of the Qur'an are both necessary and sufficient for being ushered—but only after death, resurrection, and the Day of Judgment—into the eternal presence of God.

Sufis seek union with Allah through personalized devotional love of God, which they sometimes express through music and dance, both of which are not accepted in traditional Islam. By the 13th century CE, Sufism had achieved substantial mass appeal. The Sufi movement had spread the message of Islam to many countries through missionary orders led by spiritual masters (*shaykhs* in Arabic, *pirs* in Persian) who guided their disciples through training, advice, and example. The most accomplished Sufi shaykhs were venerated as saints (friends of God) who could intercede on man's behalf.

The Shi'ah Muslims are different from both Sunnis and Sufis in some ways, and similar in other respects. The Shi'ah venerate the Fourteen Perfect Ones—the Prophet, Fatimah (his only daughter who outlived him), her husband Imam 'Ali, their sons Hasan and Husayn, and the other nine Imams. They believe in the intercessory powers of the Prophet's family and the Imams; and mark their birth and death anniversaries with religious processions, visit their tomb-shrines as pilgrimage sites, and mourn the martyrdom of Husayn in emotional public displays of pain and grief. The Shi'ah also believe that the "presently-

Hidden" Imam will return to lead the Muslim faithful at the end of time.

The mainline Shi'ah branch of Islam acknowledges twelve Imams (and is known as the Twelvers); and another sub-sect, the Ismailis, acknowledges only the first seven Imams (and is called the Seveners). A number of other Muslim sects have developed as well, within both the Sunni and Shi'ah branches of Islam. These were formed for doctrinal or other reasons, and attract relatively small numbers of followers. These sects include the Kharijites, Druzes, Mutawilah, Nusayris, Wahhabis, and Zaydis, among others, and have endured within the global Muslim community for centuries. There are important differences among them in belief and practice.

Of the more than 1.3 billion Muslims in the world today, over eighty-five percent are Sunnis. The Shi'ah number about 100 million, mostly in Iran, Iraq, and neighboring countries. Many millions follow the beliefs and practices of Sufism, though they also follow the "straight path" of Islam. In addition, there are the Ahmadiyah, Babis, and Baha'i who trace their roots to Islamic traditions and the Qur'an, but are generally not considered Muslims by traditional followers of Islam.

They are excluded because they proclaim new prophets after Prophet Muhammad (the Seal of the Prophets); and because the Baha'i consider the writings of their prophets, the Bab and Baha'u'llah, as scripture. These features are not consistent with the revelations of Allah in the Holy Qur'an, and with the teachings of Prophet Muhammad.

Chapter 10

Sikhism

CREATION AND EVOLUTION

SIKHISM TRACES ITS roots to Guru Nanak. In 1499 CE, the prophet Nanak founded a faith with novel beliefs and practices, which he taught to his disciples (Sikhs) for the next forty years. By so doing, Guru Nanak established Sikhism, now the fifth largest religion in the world, with over twenty-three million adherents.

Nanak Dev was born in 1469 CE into a Hindu family in Talvandi, a small town in Punjab, India. As a child and young adult, he was more interested in saintly rather than worldly pursuits. Through interactions with holy men he gained knowledge of Hinduism and Islam, the two religions then practiced in the community in which he lived. At age thirty, Nanak received his first revelation from the Eternal Lord (*Akal Purukh*; God or *Waheguru*) during a mystical experience along the banks of the rivulet Bein near

Sultanpur. Soon after this, he announced that he would follow "God's path," distinct from Hinduism and Islam.

To communicate God's message of universal love, moral living, and devotional remembrance of the Almighty God at all times, Guru Nanak embarked on extensive missionary travel throughout India and neighboring countries. Upon returning from his last such trip, he established the first Sikh community in Kartarpur, Punjab. Before he passed away in 1539 CE, Guru Nanak appointed his successor, Guru Angad Dev, to whom he bequeathed his book of hymns and revelations (*Gurbani*).

There have been a total of ten Sikh Gurus, including Guru Nanak. After the founding prophet, each Guru was appointed by his predecessor, in an unbroken line of succession—as one torch is lighted from the previous one. Guru Nanak's nine successors, with their year of ascending to the Guruship, were: Guru Angad Dev (1539 CE), Guru Amar Das (1552 CE), Guru Ram Das (1574 CE), Guru Arjan Dev (1581 CE), Guru Hargobind (1606 CE), Guru Har Rai (1644 CE), Guru Har Krishan (1661 CE), Guru Tegh Bahadur (1664 CE), and Guru Gobind Singh (1675 CE).

All Ten Gurus performed the prophetic function, and communicated God's message, as Guru Nanak had done. Sikhs honor, but do not worship, the ten Gurus as prophets. The Gurus were human, not divine, and their own lives showed by example what it meant to be a good Sikh.

During his missionary travels, Guru Nanak preached his message to all, irrespective of their caste, creed, or religion. His companion was Mardana, a Muslim rebeck player. Guru Nanak composed hymns in Punjabi; initiated and led congregational prayers in which everyone could participate freely; established a common kitchen (*langar*) which served everyone irrespective of caste or religion; and instituted the practice of voluntary sharing (*daswandh*) with the poor and needy. He spoke of a Loving God that cared about mankind and could be reached by following the message being conveyed through Nanak. The followers (Sikhs) of Guru Nanak (initially known as *Nanak Panthis*) were asked to lead a morally-good life in accordance with the Guru's teachings.

The next four Gurus helped firmly establish the new religion founded by Guru Nanak. They composed sacred hymns and recorded them in books (*pothis*) as Guru Nanak had done, and established the hymns (*Gurbani*) as the object of highest reverence for the Sikhs. They also established religious centers in various places in Punjab, including Amritsar, where the Sikh *gurdwara* known as Harmandar Sahib was built in about 1589 CE. The original (first) Sikh scripture was personally installed by the Fifth Guru, Guru Arjan Dev, at Harmandar Sahib in 1604 CE. Thus, this gurdwara (now also called the Golden Temple) was consecrated as the central place of worship for the Sikhs.

Guru Arjan Dev was martyred in 1606 CE in Lahore on orders of the Mughal Emperor Jahangir. His son Guru Hargobind built the *Akal Takhat* (Throne of the Timeless God) opposite the Harmandar Sahib, as the seat of temporal power of the Sikhs. He personally led the Sikhs in both the spiritual and secular aspects of the growing Sikh community; and as directed by Guru Arjan Dev, he maintained an army for self-defense. This tradition was continued by the next four Gurus.

The Ninth Guru, Guru Tegh Bahadur, undertook extensive travels in India, further consolidating the Sikh faith and its religious institutions and practices. He defended the religious rights of all, including Hindus, for which he was martyred in Delhi in 1675 CE on the orders of the Mughal Emperor Aurangzeb. The Sikh community was then led by his son, Guru Gobind Singh, who introduced a ceremony for formally-initiating Sikhs into a new *Khalsa* Order (of the Pure). He also prepared the final scripture of the Sikhs; and before his demise, transferred the spiritual authority of the Gurus to the Sikh scripture (then known as the *Adi Granth*) and their temporal authority to the *Khalsa Panth* (Sikh community).

The 239-year period of human Guruship ended with the Tenth Guru, who passed away at Nanded in 1708 CE at the hands of a Muslim assassin. Though the Guru-period had covered more than two centuries, there was a unity of spiritual essence (light, *jyoti*) that connected the ten Gurus. They all embodied the sacred mission and message first revealed to Guru Nanak. As ordained by Guru Gobind Singh (the Tenth Nanak) just before his demise, the Sikh scripture was henceforth to be accorded the status of Guru, and all Sikhs were to rely on it alone for guidance. After Guru Gobind Singh there have been no additional human Gurus of the Sikhs.

Guru Nanak's revelations and hymns, and those of five of his nine successor Gurus, are enshrined in the *Guru Granth Sahib*, Sikhism's sacred scripture. This holy text also includes some hymns of a few Bhakta *sants* (a Hindu sect) and Sufi *pirs* (a Muslim group) that were consistent with the Sikh Gurus' teachings. The original sacred scripture—the Adi Granth—was compiled and personally authenticated in 1604 CE by the Fifth Guru,

Guru Arjan Dev. It is available at Kartarpur, Punjab, and is known as the *Kartarpuri Bir*. The final Sikh scripture was prepared in 1705 CE by Guru Gobind Singh, who included in it hymns of his father, Guru Tegh Bahadur, but not his own.

As instructed in 1708 CE by Guru Gobind Singh, the *Guru Granth Sahib* is revered as the eternal Guru of the Sikhs. It uses the Punjabi language spoken by the common man during the Guru-period; and is in *Gurmukhi* script, which was especially developed for the purpose by the Second Guru. The Guru Granth Sahib contains the Gurus' hymns (*bani*) that are sung in the specified melodies (*ragas*). Its printed version is now a standard 1430 pages. Some of the hymns in the text now known as the *Dasam Granth* are by the Tenth Guru, and are included in the Sikhs' daily prayers.

BELIEFS AND PRACTICES

THE TEACHINGS OF the Sikh Gurus are embodied in the *Guru Granth Sahib* (GGS), Sikhism's only scripture. They are the sole source of spiritual guidance for Sikh beliefs, philosophy, practices, and way of life.

Sikhs worship only the One God (the Creator, *Waheguru*, the Wonderful Sovereign), and believe in His Word (*shabad*) as enshrined in the Guru Granth Sahib. The Sikh creedal statement (*mool mantra*) makes known God's Oneness, nature, and love of mankind. It says: "The One Supreme Being, Truth by name, the Creator, is without fear, without hate, eternal, never-incarnated, self-illumined, and known by the Grace of God." (GGS, p. 1)

According to the Sikh scripture, God is transcendent, loving, just, merciful, all-knowing, all-powerful, and ever-present. He is also immanent, i.e., inherent in all that He has created. "Having created the world, He stands in the midst of it and yet is separate too." (GGS, p. 937). "*Naam* extends to all creation. There is no place or space where Naam is not." (GGS, p. 4)

Sikhs do not believe that God incarnates as an *avatar*; and they do not believe in image- or deity worship. "He is the sole Creator. There is no second one." (GGS, p. 12). "God created the world and permeated it with His Light [*Naam*]." (GGS, p. 930]. "God is Self-Existent, without form, and incarnates not." (GGS, pgs. 1, 597, 1095)

God's love for mankind can be perceived and experienced by communing with and meditating upon the divine God (Naam and shabad). "Pray, link me to God." (GGS, p. 701). "He is always Benevolent." (GGS, p. 263). "Naam is the Creator of everything. To be divorced from Naam is death." (GGS, p. 603)

It is God's Will (*hukam*) that Sikhs wish to honor and follow, believing that a life devoted to the Truth, contemplation, and righteous deeds helps accumulate good *karma*. It prepares one to receive God's Grace, without which salvation is not possible, for good deeds alone are not enough. Upon achieving liberation (*mukti*) from the cycle of reincarnation, the individual soul gains entry into His divine court. "Everything happens within the ambit of his Will." (GGS, p. 1). "Final approval will be only by God's Grace." (GGS, p. 7)

The Sikh way of life emphasizes remembrance of God (*Naam japna*) at all times; and integrates secular and sacred aspects of daily living, based on its "whole-of-life" (*miri-piri*) ideology. Moral living is essential in Sikhism, for it is good deeds that matter. "Love, contentment, truth, humility, and other virtues enable the seed of Naam to sprout." (GGS, p. 955). "Without good deeds, no worship is possible." (GGS, p. 4) "It is by our deeds that we become near or away from God." (GGS, p. 8)

A life of service, equality, justice, and fairness is valued. Sikhs are asked to demonstrate personal responsibility, morality, charity, service, and tolerance. The Hindu caste system is not accepted; nor is gender discrimination. "Service in the world leads to approval in the Court of God." (GGS, p. 26). "The pride of caste leads to multifarious evils." (GGS, pgs. 1127-1128). "How can one who gives birth to kings be called inferior?" (GGS, p. 473)

Asceticism and renunciation are not considered appropriate. "One gets not to God by despising the world." (GGS, p. 962). "Truth and continence are true deeds, not fasting and rituals." (GGS, p. 841). "All yogic austerities, rituals, trance, etc., are in vain; real yoga lies in treating alike all beings." (GGS, p. 730)

The teachings (*bani*) enshrined in the Guru Granth Sahib are the basis for the Sikhs' moral commandments. Mankind's freedom of choice and personal responsibility are emphasized. "The *bani* is the Guru, and the Guru is the bani, all spiritual truths are enshrined in it." (GGS, p. 982). "Give up evil, do right, and you realize the essence of God." (GGS, p. 418)

Sikhism believes that this One God considers all mankind as one—irrespective of race, religion, gender, nationality, caste, or creed. The Oneness of God and oneness of humankind are foundational beliefs. Sikhism, though distinct from other religions, is a non-exclusionary religion, believing that all religions lead to God. "The One Lord is our Father. We are all His children." (GGS, p. 611). "The world is sick. O save it by any means You please." (GGS, p. 853)

These messages of the unity of God and of mankind, of God's benevolence and grace, and the means by which salvation can be attained were revealed to Guru Nanak and his successor Gurus. As recorded in the Guru Granth Sahib, Guru Nanak said: "I have uttered only what You, O Lord, have inspired me to utter." (GGS, p. 566). Other Sikh Gurus conveyed the same message: "Consider the *bani* of the *Satguru* the words of Truth. O Sikhs, it is the Lord who makes me convey them." (GGS, p. 308)

In terms of religious norms, Sikhism does not believe in ritual pollution, the caste system, gender discrimination, or auspicious times, places, rivers, or mountains. It does not have a separate cadre of priests that serve as intermediaries to God; and it does not make religious distinctions for any reason, believing that all humans are created equal in the eyes of God. Sikh women can lead religious ceremonies and public prayers, and can openly participate in the life of the Sikh community (*panth*). Reflecting the Sikh emphasis on equality, all devotees at a Sikh temple (*gurdwara*) sit and eat together from a common free-kitchen (*langar*), without making any distinctions based on caste or social status.

At Anandpur in 1699 CE, Guru Gobind Singh introduced a special initiation (*amrit*) ceremony for initiating Sikhs into the casteless *Khalsa* Order. Sikh males take the last name Singh, and females Kaur. Khalsa Sikhs are expected to display five symbols upon their person at all times, as an indication of their having been formally-initiated by partaking *amrit*. These "five Ks" (*panj kakke*; they all start with the letter 'k') have great symbolic value. They are unshorn hair (*kesh*), to show respect for God-given form, with adult males expected to wear a turban; wooden comb (*kangha*), for cleanliness of body and soul; small sword (*kirpan*), indicating readiness to fight oppression; steel wristband (*kara*), reminder of the eternal One God; and short breeches (*kachhehra*), emphasizing moral restraint.

All Sikh religious ceremonies (for rites of passage, such as birth, initiation, marriage, and death), and festivals (such as celebrating events in the Gurus' lives) are conducted in the presence of the Guru Granth Sahib (and not in presence of the sacred Vedic fire revered in Hinduism). Sikhs also have their own emblem that represents the Unity of God (*Ik Oankar*); and their blue or saffron flag (*Nishan Sahib*) is prominently displayed at all Sikh gurdwaras.

Sikhism's religious philosophy, beliefs, and practices thus clearly distinguish it from Hinduism and other world religions. It is not a sect of Hinduism, nor a syncretic blend of Hinduism and Islam. Sikhism differs from other faiths in its conception of God, the pathway that leads to Him, the teachings of its founding prophets, the scripture it follows, and its creed, way of life, religious beliefs and practices, and code of moral and social conduct. This has been the case since the time of Guru Nanak. Sikh beliefs have not changed since then, and have been the basis for the norms of religious and societal behavior endorsed by the Sikh community (*Panth*).

According to the Sikh Religious Code of Conduct

(*Sikh Rehat Maryada*) formally approved by the Sikh Panth in 1945 CE, a Sikh is: "Any person who faithfully believes in the One Immortal Being; the Ten Gurus, from Guru Nanak to Guru Gobind Singh; the Guru Granth Sahib; the utterances and teachings of the ten Gurus; the baptism [amrit] bequeathed by the Tenth Guru; and one who does not owe allegiance to any other religion."

Roots and Branches

THROUGHOUT THE PAST five hundred years, Sikhism has maintained its coherence and stability on the basis of the teachings of Guru Nanak and his successor Gurus, as enshrined in the Guru Granth Sahib. Over the centuries, some variations in belief and practice have occurred, but no widely-recognized sects of Sikhism have emerged.

Groups known as the Nirankaris, Namdharis, Sindhis, and Radhasoamis exist, but have relatively small followings, have a wide range of diverse beliefs, and are generally not considered Sikh sects. They believe in Guru Nanak, but also in various *sants* and *babas* (religious leaders); and the Nirankaris and Namdharis have living human gurus—which is contrary to the teachings of the last (Tenth) Sikh Guru, Guru Gobind Singh, who instructed that after him only the Guru Granth Sahib should be revered as the eternal Guru of the Sikhs.

Chapter 11

The Mormon Church and The Baha'i Faith

The Mormon Church

CREATION AND EVOLUTION

THE MORMON CHURCH was founded by the prophet Joseph Smith, Jr. in 1830 CE in upstate New York, USA. It is the second-youngest of our living religions. The Mormons believe in Jesus Christ, Son of the living God, and Savior of the world, and in the Christian Bible. They also believe that new messages from the Lord were conveyed to their prophet Joseph Smith, and that these are recorded in the *Book of Mormon: Another Testament of Jesus Christ.*

This book, revealed to/translated by Joseph Smith in the 1920s, is considered scripture, along with the Old- and

New Testaments of the Christian *Holy Bible*. In addition, Mormon beliefs are based on two later books by prophet Joseph Smith, *The Doctrine and Covenants* and *The Pearl of Great Price*. The Book of Mormon was originally translated into English from engraved plates of gold. It has fifteen books by different prophets, covering more than 530 pages, written in a style and format similar to that of the Christian Bible.

As noted in its Introduction, the Book of Mormon "is a volume of holy scripture comparable to the Bible… The book was written by many ancient prophets…on gold plates [which]…were quoted and abridged by a prophet-historian named Mormon." It includes a record of "the personal ministry of the Lord Jesus Christ among the Nephites soon after his resurrection [in about 30 CE; the Nephites had come from Jerusalem to ancient America around 600 BCE] ….After Mormon completed his writings, he delivered the account to his son Moroni, who added a few words of his own and hid up the plates in the hill Cumorah….On September 21, 1823, the same Maroni, then a glorified, resurrected being, appeared to the Prophet Joseph Smith and instructed him relative to the ancient record and its destined translation into the English language. In due course, the plates were delivered to Joseph Smith, who translated them by the gift and power of God….In addition to Joseph Smith, the Lord provided for eleven others to see the gold plates for themselves and to be special witnesses to the truth and divinity of the Book of Mormon."

After the translation of the Book of Mormon using the "seer stone" given by Maroni, the original gold plates were returned to the angel, and the prophet Joseph Smith established the new Mormon Church. In 1844 CE, he announced his intention to seek election to the office of U.S. President, but was assassinated by a violent mob in Carthage, Illinois. In 1847 CE, his disciples (apostles) went to Utah, built the famous Mormon Tabernacle, and continued to spread his message. The Mormon Church is now well established around the globe.

It is now also known formally as the Church of Jesus Christ of Latter-day Saints. This Church is considered by some believers to be a part of Christianity rather than a separate religion, though the *Book of Mormon* was revealed to prophet Joseph Smith as "Another Testament of Jesus Christ"—which the prophet considered "a volume of holy scripture comparable to the [Christian] Bible."

BELIEFS AND PRACTICES

As NOTED ABOVE, Mormons believe in the teachings of Jesus Christ as well as the teachings of prophet Joseph Smith. Before he ascended to heaven, Jesus came to the United States and personally preached to the descendents of the Jewish people who had settled there after their Babylonian exile in the 6th century BCE. The Christian doctrine of the Godhead comprised of the Father, the Son, and The Holy Ghost (the Trinity) is accepted, but with the difference that both the Father and Son have physical bodies.

According to the Mormon Church, baptism into the Christian faith is necessary for salvation; and both the living and the dead can be baptized—with a living person standing proxy for the dead. Individuals are punished for their own sins; but everyone, living or dead, may yet be saved through the atonement of Jesus Christ for the original transgression of Adam, the first man. The scriptures to be followed are the Christian Holy Bible as well as the sacred Book of Mormon revealed to prophet Joseph Smith.

Though the Mormon Church has spread to many countries, it has largely maintained its original unity. There are no widespread sects of the Mormon Church.

The Baha'i Faith

CREATION AND EVOLUTION

THE BAHA'I FAITH is the youngest of our living religions. It was founded in 1863 CE by prophet Baha'u'llah, a follower of the prophet Mirza Ali Muhammad, who was called "the Bab" (Arabic for "gate" or "door"). The Bab had taught that a *Mahdi* (Messiah) would soon appear to establish a kingdom of peace and justice on earth. The Bab was persecuted and martyred in 1850 CE by the authorities in Islamic Persia, and many of his followers were killed or jailed.

Soon after the Bab's demise, the nobleman Mirza Husayn-'Ali Nuri, one of the imprisoned followers of the Bab, received a revelation from God. He announced in 1863 CE that he was the Messiah about whom the Bab had prophesied, and took the title Baha'u'llah (Arabic for "the Glory of God"). He declared that he was the Manifestation of God awaited by the followers of all faiths.

Upon release from prison in Tehran, Baha'u'llah was banished from Persia (Iran), and spent the rest of his life in exile, first in Baghdad, then in Istanbul, and finally in the prison-city of 'Akka in Ottoman Palestine, where he passed away and was buried in 1892 CE. His extensive writings—books, letters, prayers, and meditations covering every aspect of human existence—are considered by his followers to be the revealed word of God.

Before his death, prophet Baha'u'llah appointed his eldest son, Abbas Effendi, as his successor and the "Center of His Covenant." Abbas Effendi, known to the Baha'is as Abdu'l-Baha, traveled widely to spread his father's message, and died in 1921 CE. The faith is now governed by a nine-member elected council known as the Universal House of Justice, which is infallibly guided by God, and is headquartered in Haifa, Israel.

BELIEFS AND PRACTICES

THE FOREMOST TEXT by Baha'u'llah is the *Kitab-i-Iqan*, revealed to him in 1862 CE while he was in exile in Iraq. Its English version, *The Book of Certitude* (translated from the original Persian by his grandson, Shoghi Effendi Rabbani, Guardian of the Baha'i Faith), was published in 1931 CE. Baha'u'llah's writings over a period of forty years, comprising one hundred volumes, are sacred scripture of the Baha'is. They are the direct revelation of the Word of God to the founding prophet of their new faith.

The Book of Certitude quotes extensively and almost-exclusively from the *surahs* (chapters and verses) of the *Holy Qur'an*, the sacred scripture of Islam. Occasionally it refers also to the books of Moses (the *Pentateuch*) in the *Hebrew Bible* (the Christian *Old Testament*) and to the gospels in the *New Testament* of Jesus Christ. In so doing, following the tradition of the Abrahamic religions, it proclaims the sovereignty, justice, love, benevolence, and oneness of God. It acclaims the prophets Adam, Noah, Abraham, Moses, Jesus (Son of Mary), and Muhammad; and says that they all were Manifestations of the Divine who progressively conveyed God's revelations to mankind.

It accepts too the beliefs of these religions regarding the final Day of Judgment, the general Day of Resurrection, the individual's reward of paradise/heaven, and the punishment of hell. It says that these prophets had spoken of the Messiah yet to come; and provides the hidden innermost meanings and true interpretations of the earlier holy books in light of the new messages revealed to the Bab and to Baha'u'llah, who were Manifestations of God just like the other previous prophets.

All these prophets, as Manifestations of the same God, express the same Truth, though they reveal distinct and sometimes divergent messages suited to their particular time and mission. The Baha'i scripture proclaims also that "no warrior could be found on earth more excellent and nearer to God than Husayn, son of [Imam] 'Ali", and grandson of the Prophet Muhammad—a belief that is consistent with doctrines of the Shi'ah sect of Islam. The Baha'i teachings are based on, and build upon, those of Prophet Muhammad. The prophet Baha'u'llah is the most-recent, but not the final, messenger of God. Another such prophet will not, however, come for at least a thousand years after Baha'u'llah's lifetime.

The Baha'is believe that the One God is the Creator of all things; and is eternal, omniscient, omnipresent, transcendent, inaccessible, almighty, and unknowable. He is conscious and rational, and has a Will and a purpose;

but He is not a person, nor a mindless force, and He is neither male nor female. The Manifestations of God are not equal to Him, are not of His essence, and are not God incarnate. The prophets are revealers of His Word; and in this sense, to know Them is to know Him. God has progressively revealed Himself through the prophets, who are all of equal rank.

Besides the prophets of Judaism, Christianity, and Islam mentioned in the Book of Certitude, the Baha'i accept the Bab and Baha'u'llah, as well as the prophet Zoroaster, the Buddha, and Lord Krishna as Manifestations of God. They believe that we should revere all the prophets and show genuine love and goodwill toward all religions, not with the expectation of reciprocity but as recognition of God's love for all humanity.

Baha'is also believe that God has made man in His own image, endowed him with an immortal soul, and conferred upon mankind the unique capacity to know and to love Him. We can reach God by having faith in and by following the path shown by the prophets, the Manifestations of God. Also needed are knowledge of our spiritual self, detachment from material things, purity and uprightness of conduct, and commitment to justice for all.

The Baha'i faith seeks unity and justice for all of the world's people, as part of a new world order. Baha'u'llah taught the principle of Oneness and unity—of God, of the human race, and of religion. There are no prescribed rituals or clergy; and statues, pictures, and use of musical instruments are forbidden in Baha'i houses of worship. Instead, Baha'u'llah, the religion's founder and prophet, laid down principles, laws, and institutions for a world civilization.

These emphasize the "golden rule" that honors the oneness of humanity, unity in diversity, equality of women and men, harmony of religion and science, independent investigation of the truth, universal education, elimination of extremes of wealth and poverty, an international auxiliary language, a universal currency, and an international body dedicated to world peace and composed of all nations. Baha'i teachings also give guidance on how to live a more meaningful life, focusing on spiritual rather than material wealth, the principle of moderation—following the law of God as conveyed by His latest Messenger—and commitment to honest work, service, marriage, and family, along with enjoyment of music and the arts.

All of these are in accordance with the basic principle of Oneness. In one of his last and most significant scriptures, known as the *Book of the Covenant*, Baha'u'llah revealed that the religion of God is Love and Unity. The foundation of the Baha'i faith, as of all the divinely-revealed religions, is love. Personal salvation requires faith in the Manifestation of God for this era, our own deeds, and God's love, mercy, and grace. We are responsible for choosing to love and serve God.

Roots and Branches

THERE ARE NO sects of the Baha'i Faith. Instead, the Prophet Baha'u'llah conveyed God's message, which is suitable for all of mankind in its current stage of spiritual development. His life and teachings have shown the path to be followed.

Humanity's destiny is to unite under the shelter of one universal religion which—as revealed to prophet Baha'u'llah—will be the Baha'i Faith.

Part Two

Religious Diversity, Unity, and Interaction

Chapter 12

Appreciating Religious Diversity

It is apparent from Part One of this book that all religions share some common features, and differ on others. Both their unity and diversity deserve recognition; as is done in this and the next chapter. We start with the observation that even a casual look at our scriptures and religious beliefs and practices is sufficient to raise doubts about the popular claim that "all religions are the same."

Our religions differ in many important respects, large and small. Even religions that can be grouped into "families"—i.e., the Abrahamic, Indic, and East Asian religions that trace their origin to a common prophet or place—differ from one another in key respects. Religions differ on their notion of the Creator, the nature and attributes of God, how the universe was created, what the religion stands for, what its ultimate goal is, and how this destination can be reached.

Religions differ too on the content of their sacred texts, the manner in which they are to be interpreted and followed, and their beliefs about the nature of heaven and hell, the human soul, the final Day of Judgment, and what comes after it. And despite some common elements, they ask us to follow different laws and commandments, rites and rituals, and norms of moral and social conduct.

Examples of each of these aspects are given below. The coverage is intended to be illustrative only, not comprehensive or complete. It seeks not to highlight any particular religion, but to draw attention to the broad range of beliefs embraced by our thirteen religions.

GOD AND HIS CREATION

THE CREATOR GOD. Religions differ even on this most basic aspect. The five Abrahamic religions—Judaism, Christianity, Islam, the Mormon Church, and the Baha'i Faith—as well as Zoroastrianism, Hinduism, and Sikhism believe in the Creator (God), known to us as *Yahweh*, the *Lord*, *Allah*, *Ahura Mazda*, *Brahman*, and *Waheguru*.

In contrast, Jainism and Buddhism do not believe in a transcendental Creator. They were originally atheistic religions; but now worship their founders, respectively Mahavira Jain and the Buddha, as God (or God-like). The remaining three religions—Confucianism, Taoism, and Shintoism—do not believe in a Creator God, focusing instead on the material world and the ancestral-, human-, and nature spirits that inhabit it.

The Nature of God. God, the sole Creator, is transcendent as well as immanent, loving, merciful, compassionate, and just. He has many attributes—ninety-nine Names according to Islam—and can be experienced deep within us; but is ultimately unknowable and ineffable, according to all religions. He is pure Spirit (in Hinduism); un-Created (in Zoroastrianism and Islam); and eternal, self-illumined, and without fear or hate (in Sikhism).

For Hinduism, this whole universe is Brahman; and God is infinite. Brahman's main attributes are "*sat, chit, ananda*" (Pure Being, Awareness, and Bliss); but this conception of God does not do Him justice, since He can best be described as "*neti, neti*" (not this, not this). Other religions describe God in other ways; but none of these, nor any other descriptions, can capture all aspects of the mystery that is God.

Hopefully, it doesn't really matter to God what words we use for Him (or perhaps Her) for, in essence, God is Love. This loving God is everywhere, and cares deeply about all His creation, particularly mankind. He can be reached through prayer and good deeds; and He rewards those who follow Him. On this, all religions that believe in the Creator God, agree.

Nevertheless, there still are differences. The God of Zoroastrianism, Judaism, Islam, Sikhism, and the Baha'i Faith does not incarnate; but the God of Hinduism, Christianity, and the Mormon Church, does. Hinduism's God (Brahman) incarnates as the many gods and goddesses (*avatars*, manifestations) who periodically come down to earth to help mankind; and Christianity's God (the Lord, the Father), was incarnated as Jesus Christ (His Son), and is also ever-present as the Holy Spirit. Hinduism's Trinity is comprised of Lord Brahma, Lord Vishnu, and Lord Shiva; while Christianity's Trinity is comprised of the

Father, the Son, and the Holy Spirit. These distinctions matter a great deal to Hindus, Christians, and Mormons; and so should matter to others as well.

Creation Stories. According to Genesis—the First Book of Moses in the (Jewish) *Hebrew Bible* and the (Christian) *Old Testament*—the world was made by God in six days, about six thousand years ago. Islam's *Holy Qur'an* accepts this creation story as well. The Mormon Church and the Baha'i Faith do the same.

In contrast, Zoroastrianism's *Avesta*, Hinduism's *Rg Veda*, and Sikhism's *Guru Granth Sahib* speak of the world's origin eons ago; while Jainism's *Kalpasutra* traces the first *Tirthankara* to ancient times, several million years ago. They each say how the world was created, but their stories are different; and Hinduism's sacred texts have many such stories. Other religions— Buddhism, Confucianism, Taoism, and Shintoism—refer to cosmologies that incorporate many levels of heavens, worlds, and underworlds; and each of these creation myths differs from the others.

Prophetic Revelations. The prophets, founders, revelations, and inspired teachings of a religion are of vital importance. They all differ greatly from one religion to another; and this matters a great deal. It matters to the Zoroastrians that the prophet Zoroaster received a new message from *Ahura Mazda* (God) around 1500 BCE; just as it matters to the Jews that *Yahweh* spoke in person to the prophet Moses in Hebrew on the mountain-top in Sinai during the 13th (or possibly 14th) century BCE, and to other Jewish prophets in subsequent centuries.

It matters too to Christians that *The Lord* (God) sent the Messiah, His only Son, Jesus Christ, with a new message that is now recorded in the New Testament; and that Jesus was born immaculately to the Virgin Mary through the Holy Spirit in Bethlehem in 4 BCE, was crucified in Jerusalem thirty-three years later, and was resurrected to Heaven three days after his death on the cross. And, it matters to Muslims that *Allah* conveyed the Uncreated Word through the angel Gabriel to Prophet Muhammad in Arabic in a cave on Mount Hira in 610 CE; and that these revelations continued to be received by the Prophet in Mecca and Medina for twenty-three years, until his demise in 632 CE.

Similarly, it matters greatly to Sikhs that *Waheguru* (God) revealed His divine message to Guru Nanak in Punjabi near the Bein rivulet in 1499 CE; and to his successor Gurus, until 1708 CE. For Jains, it matters that Mahavira Jain achieved omniscience by receiving the same message that the previous twenty-three *Tirthankaras* had received many centuries before him; and it matters to Buddhists that the Buddha attained enlightenment under the *bodhi* tree through intense meditation that "awakened" him to the true nature of this world.

Likewise, for the other religions. There would be no Hinduism today without the *Vedas* and other Hindu sacred texts composed and communicated by sages, seers, saints, and priests for more than three-and-a-half millennia; no Shintoism without the indigenous beliefs of Japan, centered on the *kami*; no Confucianism without the sage Confucius, and his teachings recorded in the *Analects*; and no Taoism without the seer Lao Tzu, and his *Tao Te Ching*. The Mormon Church would not exist without the prophet Joseph Smith and his *Book of Mormon*; and the Baha'i Faith would not have come into being without the prophet Baha'u'llah and his *Book of Certitude* and other sacred texts.

In all these religions, the prophet or founder—and the sacred, revealed or inspired message—were different from what had come before; and that has made all the difference.

SCRIPTURES AND CREEDS

SACRED SCRIPTURES. AN overview of the founders and scriptures of our living religions shows tremendous diversity—in terms of when these religions were founded, by whom, their main scriptures, and who authored them, when, and in what language (see Annex 1). The key beliefs of all our religions, based on their sacred texts, have been covered in Part One. The contents of various scriptures are very different.

If this were not the case, new religions would have been much harder to establish. It was only after the gospels of the *New Testament* of Jesus Christ were written that Christianity could be distinguished from the Judaism within which the prophet Jesus had preached. Most of the *Hebrew Bible* was then included in the Christian Bible—but now as the *Old Testament*, clearly marking the launch of a new message, and a new religion. The Holy Qur'an similarly provided a new message, from a new prophet, in a new scripture and language, even though it too, like Christianity, accepted some of the teachings of the Abrahamic prophets that had preceded it.

Likewise, the indigenous pagan traditions of Central Asia provided the context for Zoroastrianism, but the teachings of the prophet Zoroaster were new, and were recorded in the *Gathas*. These or similar ideas can be found in the Hebrew Bible and the *Rg Veda*, but these texts do not have an identifiable author. The origins of Judaism and Hinduism can be traced primarily to available records of their (first oral, and then) written teachings.

The early believers of what we now know as Zoroastrianism, Judaism, and Hinduism might even have shared common ancestors and cultural traditions, but once their teachings began to diverge, whole new families of beliefs emerged. The Abrahamic and Indic religions then continued to evolve over many centuries, now separated by doctrine, geography, and history. Hinduism thus became very different from both Zoroastrianism and Judaism; and this is reflected in the scriptures of these religions.

When new founders or prophets emerged on the Indian subcontinent and preached new messages, new religions were born, as in the case of Jainism, Buddhism, and Sikhism. Their scriptures reveal how different they were, from the very beginning, from the religions that preceded them or evolved alongside. The same can be said of the three religions—Confucianism, Taoism, and Shintoism—that took shape in China and Japan, for they shared a common context but gradually developed separate beliefs and identities, which are recorded in their separate scriptures. For the Mormon Church and the Baha'i Faith too, new prophets taught new messages, which they recorded in new scriptures—without which these religions might not have gained many followers.

The evolution of sects within most of our religions can similarly be traced to new beliefs and practices, some of which were then recorded in new sacred texts that now supplement the scriptures of the religion from which these sects emerged. Some of the distinguishing features of these sects have been highlighted in previous chapters. They show that it is the differences among them that give them their sectarian identity, for how else could one even consider them separate sects.

The same consideration applies to the thirteen primary religions themselves, for it is their differences that mark them as separate religions—rather than as mere sects of some "parent" religion.

Religious Creeds. Our scriptures reveal our foundational religious creeds as well. Some creedal statements are simple and straightforward, and speak directly of God. For Judaism, the creed is: "Hear, O Israel, the Lord your God is one." For Sikhism, it is: "The One Supreme Being, Truth by name, the Creator, is without fear, without hate, eternal, never-incarnated, self-illumined, and known by the Grace of God."

Some other creeds honor God as well as His Prophet, though the focus remains on God. For Islam and the Baha'i Faith, the statement is: "There is no God but Allah and Muhammad is His Prophet." For Zoroastrianism, it is: "I profess myself a worshiper of Mazda, a follower of Zoroaster, rejecting the Daevas, accepting the Ahuric doctrine; one who praises the Amesha Spentas, who worships the Amesha Spentas. To Ahura Mazda, the good, riches in treasures, I ascribe all things good."

In contrast, the Buddhist and Jain creeds make no mention of God, but focus on the founder, his message, and his key followers. The Buddhist creed is: "I take refuge in the Buddha. I take refuge in the Dharma. I take refuge in the Sangha." For Jains, it is: "I bow to the Jinas. I bow to the souls that have obtained release. I bow to the leaders of the Jain orders. I bow to the preceptors. I bow to all the Jain monks in the world."

Other creeds are more multi-faceted. For Christianity and the Mormon Church, the Nicene Creed (based on the 4th century CE interpretation of scripture) says, in part: "We believe in one God, the Father, the Almighty, maker of heaven and earth, of all that is, seen and unseen. We believe in one Lord, Jesus Christ, the only Son of God, eternally begotten of the Father, God from God, Light from Light, true God from true God, begotten not made, of one Being with the Father. Through him all things were made....We believe in the Holy Spirit, the Lord, the giver of life, who proceeds from the Father (and from the Son). With the Father and Son he is worshipped and glorified. He has spoken through the Prophets..."

For other religions, the creed is more complex, amorphous, and difficult to summarize. For Hinduism, there are many sacred texts, each thousands of verses long, and brimming with inspired mythology, philosophy, and such diversity of ideas that no statement of creed or dogma could conceivably do them justice. For Shintoism, which is based on traditional beliefs about various types of divine beings *(kami)*, the creed is difficult to pin down. A similar conclusion holds for Confucianism and Taoism, even though their main scriptures are short, succinct, and easily accessible. The Confucian *Analects* are less than a hundred pages long, and Taoism's *Tao Te Ching* fills only fifty pages—but each text is so full of meaning that it lends itself to endless interpretation.

Such difficulties notwithstanding, a religion's creed

and basic beliefs are vital, for they go to the heart of its self-identity. To say that all our religions and their creeds are essentially similar would be quite a stretch.

Goals and Pathways

The Ultimate Goal. Though God created all mankind as one, our religions lead us to different ultimate destinations. For Judaism, Christianity, and the Mormon Church the desired goal is Heaven; but for Zoroastrianism, Islam, and the Baha'i Faith, the goal is Paradise. Those admitted into Heaven or Paradise live happily and in peace, for eternity, with God; the others go to Hell. But these destinations are differently described in their respective scriptures; in the Christian Bible and the Holy Qur'an, for instance.

For the four Indic religions, the ultimate goal is spiritual liberation (*moksha*, *mukti*) from the endless cycle of rebirth (*samsara*), followed by eternal rest for the liberated soul either in union with God (for Hindus), or in His presence (for Sikhs), or in a state of *nirvana* (for Buddhists) or *moksha* (for Jains). The remaining three religions—Confucianism, Taoism, and Shintoism— seem to be less definite about the ultimate resting place, presumably because it matters less to them.

Pathways to God. Religious pathways differ; significantly. The beliefs and scriptures of every religion show us the way to reach God and our ultimate destination, but each religion charts a very different route, as discussed in Part One of this book.

For example, the prescribed Jewish way of life—in terms of its beliefs, practices, laws and commandments, rites and rituals, etc.—is different from the Christian way. And both are different from the "straight path" of Islam that is covered in considerable detail in the Qur'an, Hadith, Shari'ah laws, the "five pillars" of Islam, and the other religious practices expected to be followed by a good Muslim.

Each of these pathways is different too from the Middle Way of the Buddha; the Jain and Sikh ways of life; and the four different religious paths available to Hindus to choose from. And they are all very different from the paths expected to be followed by believers of Zoroastrianism, or of the three religions that trace their origin to countries in East Asia.

Importantly, because our ultimate destination after death is paramount, it is these pathways to God that matter most while we live. They determine what we are expected to spend our time and effort on, what we strive to do well, and occasionally what we disagree on and even fight about.

Since all these pathways ultimately lead to God—and have been revealed or inspired by Him—the differences presumably do not matter to God, and hence should not matter to us. But until we can "rise above" our own religious beliefs and consider others' religions as (equally) valid, to say that the diversity of pathways to God do not matter to us would perhaps be difficult for a "true believer" of any particular religion to accept.

THE SOUL AND ITS JUDGMENT

THE HUMAN SOUL. Our religions differ on how they conceive

of the human soul and what determines its fate. For the Abrahamic religions, the soul is pure spirit; and comes into being upon birth or perhaps soon after conception. What happens to the soul after death of a person depends only on how morally that particular life has been lived. The standards of morality and faith that apply are as per the beliefs of the religion (and sect, if applicable) of that individual.

In contrast, for Hinduism, there is a universal Pure Spirit (*Paramatman*, Brahman; a kind of "super-Soul") that always exists, of which the individual soul (*atman*) is a part, and to which it returns upon being liberated from the cycle of rebirth. In Indic religions, the moral law of *karma* (plus God's grace, in Sikhism) determines what happens to the soul after the end of each life—for the soul continues to be reincarnated in subsequent lives, whether human or non-human, until it attains spiritual liberation from the cycle of rebirth.

Jainism and Buddhism believe in a soul, *karma*, and reincarnation, but not in a Supreme Being or God on whom they rely for salvation. There is a further difference as well—in Jainism, unlike the other Indic religions, the soul that is reincarnated is not pure spirit, for it has accumulated entanglements (*karma*, spirit-in-material-existence), which must be cleansed before the soul can be liberated from the cycle of rebirth.

For the three religions—Confucianism, Taoism, and Shintoism—that do not rely on God or believe in reincarnation, the nature of the soul is still relevant, for these religions do believe in a soul that continues to exist after death. The difference is that this soul then exists as an ancestral- or nature-spirit that continues to affect and guide those still living upon this earth.

The Last Judgment. In Zoroastrianism, each spirit that has been separated from its body upon the latter's death is judged on how ethically it had lived on earth; and if the good outweighs the bad on the scale of "moral goodness," it gains entry into Paradise and is reunited with its body. Then, at the Last Judgment, all those who had ever lived are judged again by having to pass through a river of molten metal. Based on this test, the wicked perish forever, and the good live on eternally in bliss with Ahura Mazda.

In the five Abrahamic religions—though there are some differences of detail between Christianity and the ancient Judaic sects—in general, upon death of an individual, the human soul is judged by Yahweh, the Lord Jesus Christ, or Allah (as applicable) on the Last Day of Judgment, and gains entry into eternal Heaven or Paradise (for those who have been good), or is forever damned to spend eternity in Hell (for the bad). The moral standards used in making this Judgment are the ones that apply to that particular religion.

In the Indic religions, the soul is judged individually upon the death of the body. This individual soul is reincarnated many times, until it fully meets the moral standards of the religion followed by that person during his/her most-recent life, after which it attains liberation from the cycle of rebirth. Unlike the Abrahamic religions, there is no Final Day of Judgment when all souls that ever lived will be judged. This is the case for the East Asian religions as well.

Religious Laws and Tolerance

Laws and Commandments. The religious and moral

standards expected to be met by any believer during his/her lifetime and after death (when the soul is judged) are based on the expectations of the particular religion followed by that person. These standards depend in part on the laws, commandments, and principles prescribed in the relevant scriptures, and on how these have been interpreted by sages, seers, and priests in subsequent centuries, right up to the present time.

Every religion has its own laws, prescriptions, codes of moral conduct, or other expectations of social and personal behavior related to the religious aspects of life; and these differ from one religion to another. Sometimes, the sects within a religion differ on these matters too. Some of these differences have been discussed in Part One of this book.

Hence, it is important that every believer become knowledgeable about and try to follow, as far as possible, the expectations of his/her particular religion or sect—i.e., the many do's and don'ts, norms and values, rites and rituals, and practices prescribed in the relevant scriptures and other sacred texts based on them. Not doing so to the best of one's ability has large and enduring negative consequences—especially after death—that are best avoided. We cannot afford to take this responsibility lightly, whatever our religion.

Religious Tolerance. In the modern secular world-view, each of us has the same "universal" human rights, and expects to be treated equally in all respects. In the religious domain too, most scriptures teach that one must treat others as "yourself"—which means with respect, compassion, and acceptance, as well as the other kindnesses we expect from others for ourselves.

However, most scriptures, and the way they have been interpreted and used throughout history, make distinctions based on religion, gender, or caste. Such distinctions are not a trivial matter, especially those based on religion, for they have led to horrendous gender- or caste discrimination or "holy war" (e.g., the crusades; *jihads*) that have lasted centuries and damaged or destroyed millions. Furthermore, according to the scriptures of the Abrahamic religions, distinctions based on religion are important not only during our earthly-existence, but will also determine what will happen during the (second) coming of the Messiah, and where our soul will end up for eternity after the Day of Judgment.

Adherents of non-Abrahamic religions naturally follow other scriptures—which too have been revealed or inspired by God—and which provide a different view of what will happen to their soul after it leaves the human body, and on what basis it will be judged by God. As a result, it seems odd that any particular set of religious teachings could be intended by God to apply universally and equally to all mankind, especially to those humans who do not follow the "right" scriptures (however defined), or may not even be aware of them.

This apparent paradox in our scriptures is not easily resolved. Perhaps we need to accept that God's ways will forever remain mysterious for mere mortals. Our best option may be to leave the matter entirely in God's loving, merciful, and just Hands, for—according to our own sacred scriptures—what finally happens to our soul is, after all, ultimately for God alone to judge.

Chapter 13

Celebrating
Religious Unity

Our religions are not the same, but they do have some common features. Because religions are complex phenomena, it is not uncommon for reasonable people to differ on what they see when they look at any particular religion, or when they examine all thirteen living religions together, as we are doing here. If the glass is half-full of differences, it is also half-full of similarities. Switching metaphors, if one side of the religious coin displays differences, the other side shows similarities.

We can speak of the Abrahamic, Indic, and East Asian religions only because religions within each "family" are similar in so many ways, though they differ in other equally-significant ways. Sects too, within religions, share this feature. They are sufficiently different to be considered different sects, but are so similar in other ways that they are sects, not different religions.

Some similarities are even shared by all religions. These similarities stem from the common human needs that all religions seek to satisfy, and from the common divine source that most religions share. With the unity of God and the unity of mankind as their common denominator, all (or most) religious pathways can, in a sense, be said to lead to the same destination (their common source), God—even though these pathways are quite dissimilar, and all religions are definitely not "the same"(as discussed in the previous chapter).

We consider religious similarities below, focusing on some salient ones. These are the similarities within and across religious families, at the personal and community levels, in relation to God and man. Only a few examples are given for each aspect, to simply illustrate the point. The main conclusion is that there is indeed unity among our religions, despite their diversity; and that this unity—which too is God's creation—deserves to be celebrated.

UNITY AMONG RELIGIONS

UNITY WITHIN FAMILIES. The five Abrahamic religions—Judaism, Christianity, Islam, the Mormon Church, and the Baha'i Faith—have a number of identical or very similar beliefs. These include beliefs in the One God, the Hebrew Bible's creation story, the notion of (original) sin against God, the need for redemption, many (though not all) of the prophets, some (though certainly not all) of the commandments, the future coming of a Messiah (though not the same one), the expectation of a kingdom of God on earth (though not for the same set of followers), a soul that exists after death, the Last Day of Judgment, and heaven and hell.

These are not minor similarities, of little consequence. They matter a great deal, for they bind these religions into one family with common roots, beliefs, and ancestry. This does not mean that there are no differences of belief and practice among these religions; there are many—some very important and enduring, as discussed in the previous chapter. Occasionally these differences have even led to violent conflict; but the similarities are notable too, and distinguish the Abrahamic family from other religions.

Among the Indic family too—Hinduism, Jainism, Buddhism, and Sikhism—there are similarities (and of course differences). They have similar beliefs in an everlasting soul that reincarnates, in the unending cycle of rebirth, in the efficacy of deeds (though different ones) for helping achieve salvation (differently defined), and in the moral law of cause and effect (*karma*; though *dharma* differs). The Zoroastrian religion shares some similarities with both the Abrahamic and the Indic families, though there are important differences too.

Similarly, the East Asian religions—Confucianism, Taoism, and Shintoism—share some features, and differ on others. They are all deeply anchored in their respective historical and cultural contexts, believe in a world of ancestral- and nature-spirits that continuously interact with living beings, do not rely on a transcendent Being for ultimate salvation, and instead focus more on the here-and-now than on the hereafter.

Unity Across Families. Though our religions can be grouped into different families, they all share some common features too. For most religions, salvation (however defined) is the ultimate goal; and most believers expect to get there. In the Abrahamic religions, everyone gets only one chance of a lifetime (literally) to make it or break it; and there is no assurance that the destination sought will ultimately be reached, for not all humans will finally rest in peace in heaven.

For believers in the Indic religions, the ultimate goal of salvation is assured for all, for everyone gets many shots at the goal, and the process of reincarnation of an individual soul ends only when salvation is finally achieved. Despite this not-insignificant difference between the two families, the important common factor is the hope of salvation; and the assurance that if one faithfully follows the pathway prescribed in any particular religion—and with the helping hand (grace) of God in some cases—salvation (i.e., heaven or paradise or moksha or nirvana) is definitely achievable.

All religions also believe in the efficacy of prayers, rites and rituals, which are our way of directly communicating with God and seeking His help, guidance, love, compassion, and mercy. More importantly, we know that God cares for each of us, and notices every little detail of what we think, feel, and do (or do not)—though His love is apparently not unconditional, at least for some religions, since some humans will unfortunately end up in the unforgiving fires of hell. But the mere fact that He cares for mere humans is important enough to keep us going, and to sustain our belief in our religions.

Relationships with God

Following God's Will. For many religions, an intense, revelatory or mystical experience changed the heart and mind of the chosen prophet or founder. The origins of other religions are shrouded in the fogs of time or can be attributed to the unrecorded collective efforts of many individuals. The historical timing and significance of each of these "creation-stories" varies, but for every religion—without exception—the timing, content, messenger, and manner of conveying the revealed or inspired message were just right. God's message, the prophet's prophesies, the sages' sacred hymns, or the seers' wise words fell on receptive ears; and as new followers came into the fold, a new religion was established. Gradually, it evolved into the religion we know today.

Thus, what is common to all religions is that their main message resonated deeply, not only for the particular messenger but for all those for whom it was meant. Both the content of the message, and its impact on those who received and followed it, made the difference. Once the seeds of a religion were planted on ready-soil, they germinated and spread, and each religion went on to change the course of our religious history, to a greater or lesser extent.

Importantly, this did not happen by chance. The creation and evolution of all religions have been in accordance with God's Will—which we have willingly followed, for man's choice too was involved, every step of the way.

God and the Individual. We all come into this world one by one, and leave it, alone. Ultimate salvation is for the individual, not for the collective. So, it is good that in all religions, the focus is on what an individual is expected to do or not do, irrespective of what others do or not.

No religion says that achieving salvation is going to be easy. But for all religions, the rewards are great—and are achievable, if we persist, if we truly believe. This is what our religions' founders found to be true; and what they showed by the example of their own lives. Even the prophets had to work hard at it, and they often suffered; but in the end, it was worth the effort, and had huge payoffs.

The prophet Zoroaster was persecuted and assassinated; Moses spent forty years in the desert, and never reached the promised land; Jesus Christ was tortured and crucified; Mahavira Jain spent many years in solitary meditation, as did the Buddha; Confucius and Lao Tzu gained followers only towards the end of their lives; Prophet Muhammad fought many battles for his life and message; Guru Nanak contemplated deeply for many years in far-off places; Joseph Smith was killed by his enemies; and the prophet Baha'u'llah died in exile. Nevertheless, despite all these troubles, the prophets and founders persevered and succeeded, not only for themselves, but for the rest of us. They, with God's grace, showed us the pathway(s) to be followed; and these have become the basis for our living religions.

In addition, in all religions, to come closer to God, we are asked to go beyond what we (merely) believe. To connect fully with God, we are asked to relate to God not only with the head, but also with the heart; i.e., to open our hearts and minds to receiving Him and His message. Beliefs, scripture, and doctrine are important, but they have to be internalized, not just expressed through externally-visible action. We have to look within, as well as without.

A human being disconnected from the Supreme Being—i.e., one (self) without the Other (God)—feels incomplete. To bridge the gap, mysticism has its place, as does meditation. To benefit from these methods, personal devotion and dedication are needed, whatever the religion. Everyone needs to seek God not only in the inner sanctum of the temple, church, synagogue, mosque, or gurdwara, but also deep within his or her inner self. Genuine inner-peace and contentment have to be earned and learned by each seeker, individually.

God and the Community. All religions recognize that the individual needs help, not only from God, but also from his fellow man. They place emphasis on groups of individuals that support one another, whether as priests ministering to their flock, or as communities providing a sanctuary for those in need.

In some religions, numbers are important. For example, the *panj piaras* (the "five beloved ones") who signify the presence of the divine for Sikhism; and the minimum ten adult males needed for a Jewish synagogue service to be considered valid. In other cases, the community counts in other ways. The *sangha* has religious significance in Buddhism; just as the *panth* in Sikhism, the *ummah* in Islam, and the Church in Christianity play a crucial role in the practice of religion. The community sanctifies prayers in the prescribed sacred space—be it a church, mosque, temple or gurdwara; and without intense emotion-charged community participation, there would be little fervor at any religious festival or celebration.

Communal prayers are thus important for most religions. There is strength in numbers, and in the bonds thus created. In religion, as in secular life, we hang together so that we may not hang separately. Each individual at a religious service serves as a willing witness to our fellow believer's devotion to our common God. We collectively benefit from this public reaffirmation of the role of God in the religious life of our community and its members.

MORALITY AND UNITY

SHARED MORAL PRINCIPLES. Our religions help us relate not only to God, but to our fellow humans too. Every religion values certain moral principles. Many of these are common to all religions, even though some of these religions have arisen separately—in vastly different contexts of time, place, history, language, and culture.

For the Abrahamic religions, common prophets (Abraham, Noah, Moses, for example) and shared scriptures (the *Hebrew Bible*, which is Christianity's *Old Testament*) provide the basis for common commandments. Some of these commandments relate to man's relationship with God, but most provide moral guidance on the principles that should govern relationships among humans. For the Indic religions, their common geographic and cultural roots provide the basis for what is considered appropriate behavior in inter-personal and inter-group relationships, and for religiously-sanctioned attitudes and social practices. Similarly, the East Asian religions share cultural norms, and these too find continuity in the religious domain.

Remarkably, all religions share what is known as the

"golden rule"—which in simple language asks that we "treat others as we ourselves wish to be treated." They also strongly emphasize reciprocity, love, mercy, justice, compassion, fraternity, equality, and such other universal values and human rights that we now consider desirable norms for moral interpersonal and social behavior.

These values reflect our view of God as well as of ourselves. God is loving, merciful, just, compassionate, caring, forgiving, and considers us all His children. In loving us, He makes no distinctions of caste or creed, race or religion, gender or geography, history or culture. He presumably treats us all equally; and so should we. This is in our self-interest; and is also our sacred obligation as humans, made in God's image.

Hence, in the moral sphere, our religions—despite their different pathways to God—ask us to relate to each other "as one", i.e., as one mankind, making no distinctions of gender, race, religion, creed, or nationality. This is for the good of all—which is perhaps just another way of saying that it is moral, and hence finds favor with God and the religions He has created.

One God, The Creator. There can be only one un-created, self-existent, Creator—whom we call God. This One God is the source of all that exists, including our religions—and their prophets, scriptures, beliefs, practices, rites, rituals, moral principles, and everything else we consider religious.

Stated differently, all religions—including those that believe in God, as well as those that do not—have been created or inspired by God. These religions have many differences and similarities. These features, as well as the processes through which religions have been created or have evolved (discussed in Part One) are worth noting. They show that both the diversity and unity of our religions are God's creation, working through mankind.

Over the past five millennia, many prophets, sages, seers, priests, and ordinary people have played their part in the processes by which our living religions have gradually evolved to become what they are now. They have all served God; for, in essence, all of it is God's work. And this is cause for celebration.

We need to keep this simple fact in mind as we look to the future, as we do in the next chapter.

Chapter 14

Embracing Interfaith Interaction

Past Interfaith Interactions

B*ENEFITS OF INTERACTION.* Interfaith interaction is not new; religions have interacted with each other from their very beginning. The prophets and founders of our living religions were human; and though they served as God's messengers, they were influenced too by the societies and cultures in which they lived, and by other religions around them. Their followers, in subsequent centuries, adopted or adapted some religious beliefs and practices of other religions, thereby modifying—and thus helping to continually evolve—their own religion.

Many examples come easily to mind. Zoroastrianism and Hinduism share ancient cultural traditions whose traces still linger in modern times. The Zoroastrian king Cyrus provided sanctuary and support to the Jews exiled to Babylon, and in 515 BCE helped them return to Jerusalem to re-build their Temple. Jesus Christ was a Jewish preacher, and the religion that was founded after his resurrection now considers Judaism's *Hebrew Bible* as part of the *Christian Bible*. And, Islam's Prophet Muhammad interacted with Jews and Christians, and the *Holy Qur'an* accepts many of the Jewish and Christian prophets and their teachings.

Other examples: Jainism and Buddhism emerged from Hinduism around the same time in India, and were aware of each others' founders and scriptures. They have coexisted and mingled with Hinduism for millennia, and each has adapted beliefs and practices of the others. Sikhism's Guru Nanak personally interacted with Hindus, Muslims, Buddhists, and Jains during his extensive travels, and some hymns of Hindu *sants* and Muslim *pirs* are included in the Sikh scripture, the *Guru Granth Sahib.*

Similarly, Confucianism, Taoism, and Shintoism have interacted with and helped shape each other. They were greatly influenced by Buddhism too, an import from India. More recently, prophet Joseph Smith's *Book of Mormon* is "Another Testament of Jesus Christ," and his teachings are built upon a firm foundation of Christian beliefs. The Baha'i Faith recognizes but reinterprets many of the earlier prophets of Judaism and Christianity, and accepts many teachings of Islam's Prophet Muhammad and the *Holy Qur'an.*

Such inter-religious interactions, throughout history, have mostly been peaceful and mutually-beneficial. Occasionally, religious conflict has arisen too, between as well as within religions, with political and economic undertones that reflected power struggles in the religious and secular domains. These serve as a warning that unless we learn to better harness our baser tendencies, our history of religious conflict could repeat itself.

By learning appropriate lessons from the past, we could reduce our destructive attitudes and behaviors. To facilitate this process, we reflect below on how our religions have evolved from ancient times, identify some of the forces that influenced them, and consider how we might use these lessons to shape a more desirable future that increases interfaith tolerance and cooperation rather than aggravates incipient or actual conflict among our religions.

A Believer's Perspective. We begin by recalling that religions differ in many ways, yet have important similarities. In this book, we have focused on normative beliefs of various religions; and have accepted their truth claims as such. Though religious practice often falls short of desired norms, we have accepted these norms as a valid basis for appreciating and discussing the faith. Details of religious history and practice have been avoided so that salient beliefs could stand out.

We note also that this book has sought to explore religious questions from a believer's point of view. A non-believer would, undoubtedly, address various issues differently—from a different starting point, using different data and arguments, and reaching a very different conclusion—for, according to atheists, the belief in One God has one God too many, and religion is wholly man-made. The purpose here, however, has been to better appreciate all religions from their own special perspective, and to promote improved understanding among all believers.

Each of us undoubtedly has his/her own opinion about what our living religions say about God and our relationship to Him. Full agreement on such issues is unlikely; but hopefully differences of opinion can be based on a somewhat better understanding of others' positions. It is in the spirit of encouraging discussion and debate that some further thoughts are offered below. They highlight some key themes of this book, and set the stage for possible action.

REFLECTIONS ON RELIGIOUS TRADITIONS

COMMON SPIRITUAL NEEDS. As noted earlier, before the beginning of time, was the Creator, *God*. We now know this God by many names—Lord, Allah, Brahman, Waheguru, Ahura Mazda, Yahweh, etc.; but we know too that there can be only *one* such God, who has created everything that exists, including humans. And through us, He has created or inspired our religions.

This was the case during pre-historic times as well, for those humans too, and their religions, were God's creation. Though their gods were different from our gods, their Creator was the same God as ours; and their religions were as valid for them as ours are now for us. This, presumably, most believers would attest to be true; for how else could it be—there is, after all, only one Creator, who has always existed.

The story of religion began many millennia ago. For much of human existence, man lived in small tribal groups, and believed in nature gods, ancestral spirits, myths, magic, and superstitions. Prehistoric indigenous religions comprised mainly of pagan and animist traditions. These religions, along with their many gods and deities, rites and rituals, beliefs and practices, are now no more.

Ancient religious traditions were local and varied, but they were similar to one another in that they all sought to meet man's innate spiritual needs. Even when the gods were mythological and the religions different, the personal comfort they provided to individual humans were real and presumably similar—for the spiritual needs they addressed were the same everywhere.

Different Sources and Means. In all places and at all times, our ancestors attempted to make sense of the mysterious world around them, and sought support from the divine—however differently these gods may have been defined in different cultures. Because different religions had different gods, beliefs, and practices, different spiritual pathways naturally developed. These paths seldom crossed, and indigenous religions remained isolated, dispersed, and very diverse for a very long time.

As religions came and went throughout past centuries, so did the gods. New rituals and practices were introduced, and new gods came into being. The earliest civilizations relied mainly on anthropomorphic gods who seemed to be made, in some respects, in man's image. Some of these gods and goddesses fought amongst themselves, displayed anger, vengeance, jealousy, affection, and other emotions, and behaved much like men and women—though they were, above all else, divine.

The gods had a heavenly hierarchy too, which varied

from religion to religion, and changed over time. Some gods became more powerful, others morphed into other gods, and still others assumed powers and attributes that had previously been associated with other gods. Prominent among such gods were Anu, Marduk, Baal, Ishtar, Re, Rhea, Zeus, El, Agni, Mithra, and many others. There were lesser divinities and deities, angels and devils, and sacred objects and places, too. Communities were small, culture varied, religions were local, and the secular and sacred were intertwined.

Religious diversity was the norm. However, even though there were different religions at different places and at different times, all had been created by the (same) One God. Only the means adopted by God had changed over time. Indigenous religious traditions varied because they had been created at different times and places through different prophets, mystics, seers, sages, shamans, and their followers.

This was the story of our religions until about 3000 BCE. Since then, its essence has not changed, though current religions are certainly different from our ancient traditions.

CONTINUITY AND CHANGE

CREATION AND EVOLUTION. The once-vibrant religions of the past have now largely disappeared. Only their imprint on current religions remains. God's "rainbow" of religions is still there, but its colors have dramatically changed.

The religions of today were not visible at all in the glorious spectrum of God's Light in 3000 BCE. Our currently-living religions had not yet been created. The One God now known to us as Ahura Mazda, Yahweh, Brahman, The Lord, Jesus Christ, Allah, and Waheguru had not yet made Himself known to mankind in the forms we know and experience Him today. Nor had the prophets Zoroaster, Moses, Jesus, Muhammad, Guru Nanak, Baha'u'llah, and Joseph Smith yet revealed God's messages. The founders and sages Mahavira Jain, Gautama Buddha, Confucius, and Lao Tzu were yet to establish their respective religions. All these would come later, when the time and circumstance for each of them were ripe.

Over the past five thousand years, with the passage of time, the rainbow of living religions has become more and more diverse. Around 2000 BCE, God and inspired-humans introduced the colors of Zoroastrianism, Judaism, and Hinduism to the fading light of the then-existing rainbow of pre-historic religions. More than a thousand years later, Jainism, Buddhism, Confucianism, Taoism, and Shintoism were added to the holy mix of variegated religions. Some aspects of indigenous traditions continued too, but their hues were now muted. This religious spectrum did not yet have the rich colors of Christianity or Islam, which were added in the millennium that followed. And it is only in the past six hundred years that the latest religions—Sikhism, the Mormon Church, and the Baha'i Faith—were added, giving us the thirteen major religions alive today.

Continuity and change have been intrinsic to the natural process of creation and evolution of all religions. During the past five millennia, many new prophets have conveyed new messages from God. Every religion has developed new beliefs and practices. Many traditions and doctrines have been discarded or substantially modified. Fresh interpretations of previous teachings have led to reform movements and revitalization of several religions, and sometimes even to schisms that have been difficult to heal.

These processes have led to new branches and sects, particularly in Christianity, Islam, Hinduism, and Buddhism, the largest of our current religions; and to important modifications in the beliefs and practices of Zoroastrianism and Judaism, the oldest of our living faiths. The evolutionary trend has unmistakably been toward greater diversity, both among and within religions.

Unity and Diversity. As a result, our current set of living religions, and each religion within itself, now displays remarkable unity as well as diversity. The unity among religions stems from the same God that is the Creator and destination of most, if not all, living religions; and the unity within a religion stems from the original teachings of the founder or the cultural roots and traditions from which the religion draws sustenance. The diversity is due to the different messengers through which God's message has passed, and the marked variations in the spirit and mind of man that have revealed and interpreted this message through the ages.

Thus, from the One God and one humankind have come many religions; and within most religions, from one root have come many branches. Even religions—such as Jainism, Buddhism, and Confucianism—that did not initially rely on God for achieving salvation or social harmony have sought to somehow make sense of this world and the next. With the passage of time, they have invariably started treating their secular founder as a God, or at least as a bearer of a sacred message.

Though our living religions are different in many ways, there is much that is common too. For most religions, God, speaking through the prophets, is the primary source of wisdom and authority. In addition, initial revelations or inspired teachings have invariably been followed by evolutionary change in which we ourselves have played a major part.

All religions and their sects now encompass a wide range of features—myths, beliefs, practices, ways of life, paths to follow, and do's and don'ts. The unity of religions is a cause for celebration; but the diversity contains seeds of potential and actual conflict, as religious history through the ages has shown. Our current times are no exception.

To adequately respond to or preempt such conflict, we need to seriously reconsider how we think and act in relation to the "problematic" diversity among and within religions that is here to stay.

A Promising Perspective

One useful approach to dealing with conflict-producing but irreducible religious differences could be to build on the common ground that unquestionably exists among religions. We also need to frame the discussion on differences differently from the way it has commonly been done thus far. A promising perspective on respectful religious tolerance and interfaith dialogue is proposed below.

Reframing Religious Diversity. We begin with a few general observations. First, our living religions are not "the same," and never were. They are very different from one another; and each religion is becoming more diverse as time goes on and new sects are formed, in part by human hand. In the future, as has happened many times in the past, new religions might emerge or some existing ones might disappear. There is no way of knowing what God or inspired humans might do, or when. We'll just have to wait and see, with humility and compassion for all, for we won't know until it happens for whom the bell tolls. Meanwhile, let us make the most of what we have.

Second, it's worth reiterating that all religions are both God-inspired and man-made. All religions are what they are because God and we, with God's grace, have made them so. Almost all of God's messengers (prophets) who received His revelations during the past five thousand years were human, not divine. The only exceptions were the Lord Jesus Christ (the Messiah) of Christianity, and the Lords Brahma, Vishnu, Shiva, Krishna, Rama, and the many other gods and goddesses of the Hindu pantheon who are incarnations (*avatars*) of God.

The chosen prophets and inspired founders of various religions willingly communicated God's messages. Other humans then accepted their teachings and those of other sages and seers. And ordinary folk believed in and stood by their respective faiths through the ups and downs of history that followed. All religions have thus reached their present shape because of man's volition and collaborative action. We can similarly shape our collective religious future too. In so doing, we have an opportunity to maximize the good that is inherent in all religions, and root out the evil wrongly done in God's name.

Third, each religion has shown in its own way what it means to be truly human. In our attempts to be god-like or more-fully human, we have searched for God and the "self" within ourselves, in harmonious relationships with others, and in the spirit world up there and everywhere. The list and variety of our religious beliefs and practices is practically endless. Invariably, we have found spiritual sustenance, emotional comfort, and mental peace wherever and however we have looked—be it through ahimsa or asceticism, mysticism or meditation, reverence or revelation, scripture or superstition. Or for that matter, ritual or renunciation, penance or prayer, petition or pilgrimage, and in so many other ways. What we are unable to find or explain, we ascribe to the mystery that is God, for He is unknowable and ineffable. There is thus efficacy and mystery in every religion; and we are fortunate that this is so.

Fourth, sure, there are religious differences as well as similarities; but if for the skeptics the glass is half-empty, for believers it is more than half-full. All religions have been created by the same God, and they all serve our innermost spiritual needs, which are the same for everyone. The diversity is mainly because God has revealed or inspired a variety of messages to different prophets and sages, at different times and places. Both the unity and diversity have happened with God's Grace, according to His Will, and for the benefit of mankind—for the Almighty God is good, all knowing, all powerful, and merciful. We are indeed blessed, and ought to be thankful.

And fifth, religious diversity is here to stay; and we

need to come to terms with it. The different religious traditions or pathways to God show that our spiritual cravings can be satisfied in many different ways, for we humans are a varied lot, and we like variety. Neither our spiritual needs nor the religions that have arisen to satisfy them are likely to disappear any time soon. Hence, we need to find ways of getting over the seemingly-irreconcilable religious differences that now threaten the very harmony and peace of mind that could be religion's greatest gift and promise to humankind. This task is important, and we cannot afford to fail.

Embracing Respectful Religious Tolerance. Fortunately, God has already revealed a way of dealing with the diverse religions He Himself has created. An important feature of all religions is the commandment known as the "golden rule." This moral principle is often proclaimed, but seldom followed. If all of us were to genuinely "Love thy neighbour as thyself" (*Hebrew Bible*, Leviticus 19:18); or "As ye would that men should do to you, do ye also to them likewise" (Christian *Holy Bible*, Luke 6:31); or "Love your fellow men," and "Do not impose on others what you yourself do not desire." (Confucius, *the Analects*, respectively, XII.22 and XII.2), mutual-acceptance among all religions would surely follow.

Other steps are needed too. Inter-faith dialogue would have a better chance of success if we were to fully acknowledge the uniqueness and separate identity of every religion, and not focus only on what religions have in common, important though that is. For this, we need to accept the fullness of every religion, warts and all, as God-given and man-made, whether we personally believe in it or not. This would change the way we view our own religion in relation to the religions of others who do not share our faith.

Equally importantly, if we were to truly believe that *all* religions are inspired by *our own God*—the only God, the sole Creator, the creator of all souls and all religions that now exist or have ever existed or ever will—we would respect and appreciate others' religions, just as we expect them to accept and respect ours.

We would then also accept all religions as valid from their adherents' point of view, even though they obviously differ from our own or sometimes even diverge—for both the similarities and differences among religions are due to features vital to them. Some of these differences we may not easily grasp or personally value. Despite this, in appreciating and embracing religious unity and diversity, we honor our common God and recognize ourselves through the ages.

The validity of all religions follows too from our common belief in a *loving* God. The unity and diversity of our religions has been created by Him, through and for mankind. An all-loving, all-good, and all-powerful God would not mislead His followers. He would not allow *any* of our religions to go astray on a matter as important as our pathway to Him. A caring, compassionate, merciful, and just God would not have created or inspired any religion that does not lead to Him—or to salvation, heaven, paradise, moksha, nirvana, "fully-humanness", or however else we define our ultimate resting place in the presence of the Supreme.

Genuine belief in "One God and one humanity" must therefore go hand in hand with enhanced religious literacy and tolerance, and greater appreciation of the unity and diversity of our religions. Interfaith interaction could then be a rewarding experience for all, and not a frustrating zero-sum game it sometimes seems to be. Mutual understanding and acceptance would be its goal. We would converse not to convert or to score vacuous points but to better understand other religions, and to help others do so too.

For this, our hearts and minds need to be open not only to our own religion but to others' as well. All religious faiths would then be seen as equally valid in the eyes of God; and equally worthy of respect in the eyes of man.

Our belief in *The One Loving God* requires no less. It would be wonderful if we could act accordingly, for God's sake and ours.

Annex 1:

The Founders and Scriptures of Our Living Religions

(in rough chronological order)

Religion	Founder(s)	Founder Dates	Scriptures
1. Zoroastrianism	Zarathusthra (Zoroaster)	Around 1500 BCE	The *Gathas*; and the *Avesta*
2. Judaism	Prophets Abraham, Noah, and Moses	From before/ around 1400 BCE; various dates	*Torah* (the Hebrew Bible); and the *Talmud*
3. Hinduism	Various Hindu saints and seers (identities unknown)	Various dates; before/ around 1400 BCE to around 300 BCE (for the ancient sages and seers)	The *Vedas*, *Upanishads*, *Puranas*, *Brahmanas*, (and various other later texts)
4. Jainism	Mahavira Jain (and the 23 previous *Jinas*/ *Tirthankaras*)	Around 599-527 BCE	The *Puravas* (Old Texts), *Kalpasutra*, *Tattvartha-sutra*, and other sacred texts

Author(s)	Scripture Dates	Language of the Scriptures
Zoroaster (for the *Gathas*); his later disciples (for the *Avesta*)	Many centuries of oral traditions; written from 6th -9th century CE	Old Avestan, and New Avestan; later translated
Disciples of various ancient prophets (the revelations were recorded by them)	Many centuries of oral traditions; written from 8th century BCE -7th century CE	Hebrew, Aramaic (languages of the Jewish Prophets and early Jews)
Various sages, philosophers, and reformers (originally based on ancient oral traditions and teachings)	Many centuries of oral traditions, later written; the *Vedas*: 1300-800 BCE; *Upanishads*: 800-200 BCE; the *Puranas* and the *Brahmanas*: 800-500 BCE; the *Bhagavad Gita*: around 300 BCE	Sanskrit (language of Brahmin priests in ancient India); later translated
Various disciples (based on ancient oral traditions and teachings)	Based on oral traditions, written in the 3rd or 2nd century BCE; 300 years after Mahavira Jain	Ardha-Magadhi, Prakrit (the language of Mahavira); and Sanskrit (language of later priests)

Religion	Founder(s)	Founder Dates	Scriptures
5. Buddhism	Gautama Buddha	Around 563-483 BCE	The *Tipitaka*, and various other sacred texts
6. Confucianism	Kung Fu-tzu (Confucius)	Around 551-479 BCE	The *Lun yu* (the *Analects*)
7. Taoism	Lao Tzu	Around 604 BCE- 680 BCE	*Tao Te Ching* ("The Way and its Power")
8. Shintoism	Various traditional priests	Around 500 BCE—9th century CE	Various traditional texts and tracts, including the *Lotus Sutra*
9. Christianity	Jesus Christ	Around 4 BCE- 30 CE	The *Holy Bible* (including the *Old Testament* (Hebrew Bible) and the *New Testament*

Author(s)	Scripture Dates	Language of the Scriptures
Various disciples (based on ancient oral traditions and teachings)	Several centuries after the Buddha's death; based on oral traditions and teachings	Pali (language of the Buddha and his monks); and Sanskrit (language of later priests)
Disciples of the sage Confucius; other followers	Some centuries after Confucius' death	Chinese; later translated
Followers of the sage Lao Tzu	3rd century CE; based on oral traditions	Chinese; later translated
Various Shinto priests and sages	Around 5th century BCE-9th century CE; based on oral traditions and teachings	Japanese; later translated
Disciples and early followers of Christ (the prophet Jesus did not leave a written record)	Many decades and centuries after Jesus Christ's death; various versions and translations during the next 1600 years	New Testament originally in Greek, 2nd-4th century CE; in Latin, 4th century CE; in English 14th century CE; and the latest King James' version in 1611 CE

Religion	Founder(s)	Founder Dates	Scriptures
10. Islam	Prophet Muhammad	570-632 CE	The *Holy Qur'an*
11. Sikhism	Guru Nanak, and his nine successor Gurus	Guru Nanak: 1469-1539 CE; the Sikhs' Ten Gurus: 1469-1708 CE	The *Guru Granth Sahib*
12. The Mormon Church	Prophet Joseph Smith	Around 1800-1844 CE	The *Book of Mormon*; the *Doctrine and Covenants*; and the *Pearl of Great Price*
13. The Baha'i Faith	The Bab; and Baha'u'llah (the "Glory of God")	Around 1830-1892 CE	*The Book of Certitude*; and *The Book of the Covenant*

Author(s)	Scripture Dates	Language of the Scriptures
The Prophet (revelations were dictated to key disciples)	610-632 CE, and about 20 years after Prophet Muhammad	Arabic (the language of the Prophet and his followers)
The Sikh Gurus (the revelations were written and authenticated by the Gurus themselves)	The *Adi Granth*, compiled by Guru Arjan Dev in 1604 CE; the *Guru Granth Sahib* compiled by Guru Gobind Singh in 1705 CE	Punjabi (the language of the Sikh Gurus and Punjabis); written in the Gurmukhi script
Joseph Smith, the prophet himself	Translated by Joseph Smith, in 1823-1844 CE; from engraved gold plates using a "seer stone"	English
Baha'u'allah, the prophet himself	Various texts written in 1863-1892 CE by Baha'u'llah	Persian; later translated

Select Bibliography

S<small>ACRED</small> S<small>CRIPTURE</small>S

1. *The Torah—the Five Books of Moses.* Philadelphia: The Jewish Publication Society, a new translation, 1992.

2. *Hindu Scriptures.* Edited and translated by Dominic Goodall. London: Phoenix Press, 2005 (first published by J. M. Dent in 1996). Includes the *Bhagavad Gita* and other texts.

3. *The Bhagavad Gita.* Translated by Eknath Easwaran. Tomales: Nilgiri Press, 1985.

4. *The Analects.* Confucius. Translated by D. C. Lau. London: Penguin Classics, 1979.

5. *The Tao Te Ching.* Translated by Stephen Mitchell. New York: Harper Perennial Modern

Classics, a new English version, 2006 (first published in 1988).

6.   *The Holy Bible.* Authorized (King James) version. Philadelphia: National Publishing Company, 1978.

7.   *The Holy Qur'an.* Text and translation by 'Abdullah Yusuf 'Ali. Kuala Lumpur: Islamic Book Trust, 1994.

8.   *The Guru Granth Sahib.* Various translations; there is no standard version in English.

9.   *The Book of Mormon—Another Testament of Jesus Christ.* Salt Lake City: The Church of Jesus Christ of Latter-day Saints, 1981 (first published in 1830).

10. *The Book of Certitude. (The Kitab-i-Iqan).* The Writings of Prophet Baha'u'llah. Translated by Shoghi Effendi. Wilmette: Baha'i Publishing, 2003 (first published in 1931).

WORLD RELIGIONS

11. Armstrong, Karen. *A History of God—The 4,000-Year Quest of Judaism, Christianity and Islam.* New York: Ballantine Books, 1993.

12. Bowker, John, ed. *The Cambridge Illustrated History of Religions.* Cambridge: Cambridge University Press, 2002.

13. Bowker, John. *World Religions.* New York: DK Publishing Inc., 1997.

14. Breuilly, Elizabeth, Joane O'Brien, and Martin Palmer. *Religions of the World—the Illustrated Guide to Origins, Beliefs, Traditions, & Festivals.* New York: Facts on File, Inc, 1997.

15. Coogan, Michael D., gen. ed. *The Illustrated Guide to World Religions.* New York: Oxford University Press, 2003.

16. Cunningham, Lawrence S. and John Kelsay. *The Sacred Quest: An Invitation to the Study of Religion.* New Jersey: Pearson Prentice Hall, 4th ed., 2006.

17. *Great Religions of the World.* Washington, D. C.: National Geographic Society, 1978.

18. Hinnells, John R. *Handbook of Living Religions.* London: Penguin Books, 1997.

19. Hitchcock, Susan Tyler, with John L. Esposito. *Geography of Religion—Where God Lives, Where Pilgrims Walk.* Washington, D.C.: National Geographic Society, 2004.

20. Mead, Frank S., Samuel S. Hill, and Craig D. Atwood. *Handbook of Denominations in the United States.* Nashville: Abingdon Press, 12th ed., 2005 (first published in 1951).

21. Miller, John and Aaron Kenedi, eds. *God's Breath—Sacred Scriptures of the World.* New York: Marlowe & Company, 2000.

22. Noss, David S. *A History of the World's Religions.* New Jersey: Prentice Hall, 10th ed., 1999.

23. Novak, Philip. *The World's Wisdom—Sacred Texts of the World's Religions*. New York: HarperCollins Publishers, 1995.

24. Oliver, Paul. *Teach Yourself World Faiths*. Chicago: McGraw Hill, 2001.

25. Oxtoby, Willard G. *World Religions—Eastern Traditions*. Ontario: Oxford University Press, 2nd ed., 2002.

26. Oxtoby, Willard G. *World Religions—Western Traditions*. Ontario: Oxford University Press, 2nd ed., 2002.

27. Parrinder, Geoffrey, ed. *World Religions—From Ancient History to the Present*. New York: Facts On File, Inc., 1985 (first published in 1971).

28. Prothero, Stephen. *Religious Literacy: What Every American Needs to Know—And Doesn't*. New York: HarperCollins Publishers, 2007.

29. Smith, Huston. *The Illustrated World's Religions*. New York: HarperCollins Publishers, 1995.

30. Smith, Huston. *The World's Religions—Our Great Wisdom Traditions*. New York: HarperCollins Publishers, 1991.

31. Wade, Nicholas. *Before the Dawn—Recovering the Lost History of Our Ancestors*. London: Penguin Books, 2006.

Zoroastrianism

32. Boyce, Mary. ed. and trans. *Textual Sources for the Study of Zoroastrianism*. Chicago: The University of Chicago Press, 1990 (originally published by Manchester University Press in 1984).

33. Boyce, Mary. *Zoroastrianism—their Religious Beliefs and Practices*. Oxon: Routledge, 2001 (first published in 1979).

34. Carter, George William. *Zoroastrianism and Judaism*. Boston: The Gorham Press, 1918.

Judaism

35. Alexander, Philip S. ed. and trans. *Textual Sources for the Study of Judaism*. Chicago: The University of Chicago Press, 1990 (originally published by Manchester University Press in 1984).

36. Klinghoffer, David. *Why the Jews Rejected Jesus*. New York: Doubleday, 2005.

37. Robinson, George. *Essential Judaism—A Complete Guided to Beliefs, Customs, and Rituals*. New York: Pocket Books, 2000.

38. Schniedewind, William M. *How the Bible Became a Book—the Textualization of Ancient Israel*. New York: Cambridge University Press, 2004.

Hinduism

39. Bhaskarananda, Swami. *The Essentials of Hinduism—A Comprehensive Overview of the World's Oldest Religion*. Seattle: Viveka Press, 2nd ed., 2002.

40. Bryant, Edwin. *The Quest for the Origins of Vedic Culture—the Indo-Aryan Migration Debate*. New York: Oxford University Press, 2001.

41. Flood, Gavin. *An Introduction to Hinduism*. New York: Cambridge University Press, 1996.

42. Kanitkar, V. P. and W. Owen Cole. *Teach Yourself Hinduism*. Chicago: McGraw-Hill, 1995, 2003.

43. Narayanan, Vasudha. *Hinduism*. New York: Oxford University Press, 2004.

44. Nikhilananda, Swami. *Hinduism—Its Meaning for the Liberation of the Spirit*. New York: Ramakrishna-Vivekananda Center, 1992 (first published by Harper & Brothers in 1958).

45. O'Flaherty, Wendy Doniger, ed. and trans. *Textual Sources for the Study of Hinduism*. Chicago: The University of Chicago Press, 1990 (originally published by Manchester University Press in 1988).

46. Radhakrishnan, S. *The Hindu View of Life*.

New Delhi: HarperCollins Publishers India
Pvt. Ltd., 1993 (first published in 1927).

47. Sen, Kshiti Mohan. *Hinduism.* London:
Penguin Books, 2005 (first published by
Pelican Books in 1961).

48. *The Law Code of Manu.* A new translation by
Patrick Olivelle. New York: Oxford University
Press, 2004.

JAINISM

49. Jaini, Padmanabh S. *The Jaina Path of
Purification.* Delhi: Motilal Banarsidass
Publishers Pvt. Ltd., 1998.

50. Long, Jeffery D., *Jainism.* New York: I. B.
Tauris & Co. Ltd., 2009.

BUDDHISM

51. Armstrong, Karen. *Buddha.* New York:
Penguin, 2001.

52. *Dhammapad—Annoted & Explained.*
Annotated by Jack Maguire, and translated
by Max Muller. Mumbai: Jaico Publishing
House, 2003.

53. Smith, Huston and Philip Novak.
Buddhism—A Concise Introduction. New
York: HarperCollins Publishers, 2003.

CHRISTIANITY

54. Ehrman, Bart D. *Misquoting Jesus: The Story Behind Who Changed the Bible and Why.* New York: HarperCollins Publishers, 2005.

55. Fitzgerald, Michael L. and John Borelli. *Interfaith Dialogue—A Catholic View.* New York: Orbis Books, 2006.

56. George, Timothy. *Is the Father of Jesus the God of Muhammad?* Grand Rapids: Zondervan, 2002.

57. Hedrick, Charles W. *When History and Faith Collide: Studying Jesus.* Peabody, MA: Hendrickson Publishers, 1999.

58. Knitter, Paul F. *Without Buddha I Could not be a Christian.* Oxford: Oneworld Publications, 2009.

59. Segal, Alan F. *Rebecca's Children—Judaism and Christianity in the Roman World.* Cambridge: Harvard University Press, 1986.

60. Shanks, Hershel. *Christianity and Rabbinic Judaism—A Parallel History of Their Origins and Early Development.* Washington, D. C.: Biblical Archeology Society, 1992.

ISLAM

61. Al Faruqi, Isma'il R. *Islam.* Beltsville: Amana Publications, 3rd edition, 1995/1415 AH.

62. Aslan, Reza. *No god but God—the Origins, Evolution, and Future of Islam*. New York: Random House Trade Paperbacks, 2005.

63. Esposito, John L. *Islam—the Straight Path*. New York: Oxford University Press, 3rd ed. 2005.

64. Farah, Caesar E. *Islam—Beliefs and Observances*. New York: Barron's, 7th ed. 2003.

65. Rippin, Andrew and Jan Knappert, eds. and trans. *Textual Sources for the Study of Islam*. Chicago: The University of Chicago Press, 1990 (originally published by Manchester University Press in 1986).

SIKHISM

66. Cole, W. Owen and Piara Singh Sambhi. *Sikhism—Beliefs and Practices*. New Delhi: Adarsh Books, 1999.

67. Grewal, J. S. *Historical Perspectives on Sikh Identity*. Patiala: Punjabi University, 1997.

68. Kalsi, Sewa Singh. *Simple Guide to Sikhism*. Kent: Global Books Ltd, 1999.

69. Mann, Gurinder Singh. *Sikhism*. New Jersey: Prentice Hall Inc., 2004.

70. Mann, Jasbir Singh and Kharak Singh, eds. *Recent Researches in Sikhism*. Patiala: Punjabi University, 1992, 2nd ed. 2002.

71. McLeod, W. H., ed. and trans. *Textual Sources for the Study of Sikhism*. Chicago: The University of Chicago Press, 1990 (originally published by Manchester University Press in 1984).

72. Nabha, Kahn Singh. *Ham Hindu Nahin* ("We are not Hindus"), 1898 in Hindi, then in Punjabi trans. Amritsar: Shiromani Gurdwara Prabandhak Committee, 5th ed. 1981.

73. Sachdeva, Paramjit Singh. *Appreciating Sikhism*. New Delhi: UBSPD, 2008.

74. Shiromani Gurdwara Parbandhak Committee (SGPC). *Sikh Reht Maryada* (1945). English trans. Amritsar: SGPC, 2002.

75. Singh, Daljeet and Kharak Singh, eds. *Sikhism: Its Philosophy and History*. Chandigarh: Institute of Sikh Studies, 1997.

76. Singh, Harbans. *Guru Nanak—and Origins of the Sikh Faith*. Bombay: Asia Publishing House, 1969.

77. Singh, Khushwant, trans. *Hymns of the Gurus*. New Delhi: Penguin Books, 2003.

78. Singh, Nikky-Guninder Kaur. *The Name of My Beloved—Verses of the Sikh Gurus*. New Delhi: Penguin Books, 2001.

79. Singh, Patwant. *The Sikhs*. New Delhi: Rupa & Co., 2004.

The Mormon Church

80. Robinson, Stephen E. *Are Mormons Christians?* Salt Lake City: Bookcraft, 1991.

The Baha'i Faith

81. Bowers, Kenneth E. *God Speaks Again—An Introduction to the Baha'i Faith.* Wilmette: Baha'i Publishing, 2004.

82. Smith, Peter. *A Concise Encyclopedia of the Baha'i Faith.* Oxford: Oneworld, 2000.

Index

A

Abraham, prophet of the Abrahamic religions, 16, 35

Adharma, moral lawlessness, in Hinduism, 54

Adi Granth, the original (first) Sikh scripture, prepared by the fifth Sikh Guru, Guru Arjan Dev, 128

Advaitya, the non-dualistic philosophy of the unity of the Creator and His Creation, in Hinduism, 58

Agni, the god of sacrificial fire, in Vedic Hinduism, 48, 49, 60

Ahimsa, non-violence, in Jainism, 68

Ahura Mazda, the God, in Zoroastrianism, 16, 25, 27

Akal Takhat, the "Throne of the Timeless God", opposite the Harmandar Sahib gurdwara, in Amritsar, 127

Ali, the son-in-law of Prophet Muhammad, and the fourth Caliph, whose followers constitute the Shi'ah sect of Islam, 121

C

D

Dalai Lama, the head of Tibetan Vajrayana Buddhism, 84

Darshan, reverential sighting of the deity, in the Indic religions; in Hinduism, 58; in Jainism, 71

Dasam Granth, the book containing some hymns of the tenth Sikh Guru, 129

Daswandh, practice of voluntary sharing (ten percent of income), in Sikhism, 127

Dates of our religious scriptures, 189, 191, 193

David, the second King of Israel, who captured Jerusalem in 1000 BCE, 36

Dharma, the Hindu religious duties and way of life, 51, 56; the Buddhist way of life, 85

Doctrine and Covenants, sacred text of the Mormon Church, 136

Dukha, suffering, in Buddhism, 76

Dvaitya, the dualistic philosophy of the distinctness of God from His creation, in Hinduism, 58

E

East Asian religions, 21

F

Founders of our living religions, 188, 190, 192

G

Gathas, hymns of prophet Zoroaster, Zoroastrian scripture, 16, 25, 30

Gautama Buddha, the Enlightened One, (born as Siddhartha Gautama), the founder of Buddhism, 19, 65-66, 75, 76

Gilgamesh epic, 11

Gospels, the Good news of Christ's life, the four books ascribed to Jesus's disciples Matthew, Mark, Luke, and John, 101

Greco-Roman pantheon, 13-14

Greek, the language in which Jesus read and taught the Hebrew Bible, and in which the Gospels and much of the New Testament (of Jesus Christ) was written, 37

Grihastha, householder, the second stage (ashrama) of life, in Hinduism, 56

Gurbani, the revelations and inspired hymns recorded in the Guru Granth Sahib, the scripture of Sikhism, 126, 127

Gurdwara, a Sikh place of worship (temple), 127, 132

Gurmukhi, the script in which the Guru Granth Sahib, the scripture of Sikhism is written (the language is mainly Punjabi), 129

Guru Granth Sahib, Sikhism's scripture, revered as the eternal Guru of the Sikhs, 20, 128, 129

Guru Nanak, the prophet and founder (and the first Guru) of Sikhism, 20, 125-127

H

Hadith, the Prophet Muhammad's sayings and actions that

J

K

L

M

N

Nirvana, the state of blissful "no-self" and the end of desire, the goal of Buddhism, 75, 78, 79, 80, 85

Nishan Sahib, the blue or saffron colored Sikh flag displayed at all gurdwaras, in Sikhism, 133

Noah, prophet of the Abrahamic religions, 16, 35

O

Old Testament, the part of the Holy Bible, the Christian scripture, that is from the Hebrew Bible, Judaism's scripture, 39, 101, 102

P

Pali, the language of the earliest canon of Buddhism, 77

Paramatman, the Universal Atman or Spirit, in Hinduism, 55; a "super-Soul" in Jainism, 70

Parsva, the 23rd Tirthankara, in Jainism, 72

Paul, the disciple of Jesus Christ who helped found the Christian Church, 100

Pearl of Great Price, sacred text of the Mormon Church, 136

Pentateuch, the first five books of the Hebrew Bible ascribed to prophet Moses, also called the Torah or Written Law of Judaism, (the books are Genesis, Exodus, Leviticus, Numbers, and Deuteronomy), 38-39

Persian civilization, 14

Pirs, members of the Sufi (Muslim) group, 128

Pothis, books in which Guru Nanak and his successor Gurus recorded their hymns (Gurbani), 127

Q

R

S

T

U

Z

Also available, by the same author

Appreciating Sikhism

About the Book:

Who is a Sikh? Are Sikhs Hindus? Is Sikhism a blend of Hinduism and Islam? How does Sikhism differ from other religions?

In clear and simple language, this brief essay "Appreciating Sikhism" provides answers. Sikhism's beliefs and practices are outlined in relation to Buddhism, Christianity, Hinduism, Islam, Jainism, and Judaism. Their common features and differences are noted, but no religion is shown to be better than any other. They are just different—and the differences are significant.

In four relatively self-contained parts, each with a clear focus, this book covers key Sikh beliefs, practices, philosophy, and history, drawing on the latest publications. Succinct Tables and Annexes provide supplementary information. The writing style is non-academic; and original color photographs bring the subject to life. The reader is invited to build on this insightful introduction to Sikhism, and to help others do so as well.

Book details: ISBN 978-81-7476-583-3, paperback, 241 pages, published in 2008 by UBS Publishers' Distributors, New Delhi.

Available from www.Amazon.com and other websites, including www.ubspd.com and www.gobookshopping.com